M

College students enjoy a meal at a White Castle. During the 1930s, Billy Ingram shrewdly built his White Castles near universities and colleges. Tom Monaghan followed the same strategy 30 years later when starting his Domino's pizza chain.

BUSINESS BUILDERS
IN FAST FOOD

Nathan Aaseng

The Oliver Press, Inc.
Minneapolis

The Oliver Press, Inc.
Charlotte Square
5707 West 36th Street
Minneapolis, MN 55416-2510

Library of Congress Cataloging-in-Publication Data
Aaseng, Nathan.
Business Builders in Fast Food / Nathan Aaseng
p. cm. — (Business builders ; 3)
Includes bibliographical references and index.
  Summary: Profiles ten entrepreneurs who started fast food busi-
nesses, including Fred Harvey (Harvey House), Walter Anderson
and Billy Ingram (White Castle), J. F. McCullough and Harry Axene
(Dairy Queen), Maurice and Richard McDonald and Ray Kroc
(McDonald's), Harland Sanders (Kentucky Fried Chicken), and Tom
Monaghan (Domino's Pizza).
ISBN 1-881508-58-7 (library binding)
1. Restaurateurs—United States—Biography—Juvenile
literature. 2. Fast food restaurants—United States—History—
Juvenile literature. 3. Businesspeople—United States—Biography—
Juvenile literature. [1. Restaurateurs. 2. Fast food restaurants—
History 3. Businesspeople.] I. Title. II. Series.
TX910.3.A27 2000
338.7'6164795'092273—dc21
[B]   99-086888
                           CIP
                           AC

ISBN 1-881508-58-7
Printed in the United States of America
07 06 05 04 03 02 01   8 7 6 5 4 3 2 1

CONTENTS

INTRODUCTION

FROM TAVERNS TO TAKE OUTS

Most Americans in colonial times never ate anything but home-cooked meals their entire lives. When they sat down to dinner, they did so either at their own residence or at the home of a friend, neighbor, or relative. They dined out at church socials, weddings, or funerals where home-cooked food was also served. But the idea of entering a place of business to eat a dinner prepared by strangers would have sounded terribly unappealing to them. Such meals were for travelers only and were considered one of the worst hazards of traveling.

TAVERN MEALS

No one in the 1700s operated a business exclusively to serve food. Travelers found meals in taverns or

Built in 1770, the William Pitt Tavern in Portsmouth, New Hampshire (top), was typical of the era. The interior of a colonial tavern is reproduced at Williamsburg, Virginia, in the Raleigh Tavern.

inns. As a sideline to their main business, some tavern owners would provide the bare minimum in services to travelers. They might offer rooms where travelers could sleep (as many as five to a bed) and perhaps an evening meal. But the bell rang only once for supper, and travelers who were not present when it was served missed out.

By most accounts, missing a tavern dinner was no loss. Not many people had the time or money to travel, so there was little incentive for tavern owners to cater to those few who did. Tavern owners had no reason to go to the expense and effort of preparing delicious meals for occasional customers.

EATING HOUSES AND RESTAURANTS

At the very end of the eighteenth century, the country's growing population and improvements in roads and transportation services contributed to increased travel in the eastern United States. More travelers meant that more hungry strangers in need of meals were passing through towns and cities. Some enterprising business people decided that the demand for meals had grown high enough that they could make a living filling it. The first places that specialized in serving cooked food in the United States were known simply as "eating houses." Along the East Coast, they were often called "oyster houses" because oysters were commonly served.

In the early 1800s, some eating house operators who wanted to improve their public image called their establishments restaurants. This variation of a French word, *restaurer*, means "to restore." They wanted to project the idea of weary, hungry people being "restored" by their meals.

The first well-known restaurant in the United States was Delmonico's on Manhattan Island in New York. John Delmonico, a former sea captain, emigrated from Switzerland to New York, where he opened a wine shop in 1827. With the help of his brother, Peter, a pastry chef, he began serving coffee and pastries to his customers. The Delmonico

Chefs cooking in Delmonico's huge kitchen about 1902

Lorenzo Delmonico (1813-1881)

brothers were so successful that they asked their nephew, Lorenzo, to join the business. By 1835, the family had converted their operation to a fancy, full-scale restaurant. There was no such thing as a set menu at Delmonico's. The day's fare was either written on a chalkboard or else the waiters simply told customers what was available. The success of Delmonico's inspired many of the finest hotels in large cities, such as the Palmer House in Chicago and the Parker House in Boston, to establish their own dining rooms.

Restaurant owners, however, had trouble duplicating Delmonico's success. The vast majority of Americans could not afford to eat at these high-class restaurants. Competition for the small segment of the population that could grew so fierce that most restaurants closed shortly after they opened. Others moved constantly from place to place in hopes of finding a location that could attract the customers they needed. The results of a survey of restaurants in Charlestown, Massachusetts, were typical of urban areas. It found that fewer than half of the restaurants open in 1858 were still in business at the same place with the same owner just two years later.

PORTABLE MEALS

Meanwhile, the industrial revolution and the growth of cities created a demand for a different kind of eating place—one that would serve meals that the average worker could afford. Prior to the industrial age, virtually everyone worked close enough to home

to return there for the noon dinner, which was tra-
ditionally the largest meal of the day.

That changed when industrialists in the north-
eastern cities built huge factories and hired hundreds
of people to work various shifts. Many workers had
to travel several miles to get to the factories. Others
lived in boarding houses that served meals only at set
times of the day. Workers no longer had time to
return home for dinner and then rush back to the
factory to continue their work day. Factory owners
did not typically provide a place for the workers to
eat. So many workers just sat on the ground or floor,
eating whatever they had brought from home. For

This illustration of mill workers in New England appeared in Harper's Weekly *in 1868. Most carry buckets or baskets of food brought from home to eat during what were often 12-hour workdays.*

people who were used to the noon dinner being the main meal of the day, this was highly unsatisfactory.

Enterprising food vendors realized they could do a good business by bringing a hot dinner to the workers. At first they loaded up small carts and pushed them to the factory gates every noon. The pushcart vendors were limited to foods that required little preparation and could be easily eaten without a table and utensils. Sandwiches, sausages, and pies were ideal portable meals.

German immigrant Charles Feltman, for example, made a living selling pies from a street stand in Coney Island, New York. In 1867, he decided he could do better setting up a portable lunch cart. He served his favorite easily prepared, convenient-to-eat meal—a bland German-style sausage served on a white bread roll. Feltman's sausages became a huge favorite among workers in New York.

Charles Feltman's version of the hot dog became so popular that in 1901 he set up an enormous restaurant on Coney Island that specialized in hot dogs and employed 1,200 waiters. His marketing efforts were so successful that many Americans still refer to hot dogs as Coney Islands.

Similar sausage sandwiches began appearing in many cities, taking their names from the towns in which the recipes were said to have originated. Sandwiches from Frankfurt, Germany, were called frankfurters; those from Wien—or Vienna, Austria—became known as wieners. Chicago cartoonist Tad Dorgan inspired the most common name for this food when he drew a picture of a dachshund in a bun. From that moment, the greatest food fad of the late 1800s became known as the hot dog.

FROM CARTS TO WAGONS TO DINERS

As more and larger factories continued to open in big cities, the demand for convenient, portable noon

Hot dog vendors became a common sight on city streets.

meals continued to grow. Before long, vendors switched from food carts to horse-drawn wagons to haul in their food. Some of these served thousands of hungry workers every day.

Always looking to increase their profits, lunch wagon owners started to keep their food wagons open for business even after the noon rush. People who lived near the factories could stroll over to the lunch wagon at almost any time of day or night and get a bite to eat. While the volume of business was light compared to the factory lunch breaks, the longer hours provided extra income during times when the lunch wagons used to sit idle.

Lunch wagons stayed open so long in one spot that there was no longer any reason for them to be on wheels. The owners found they could save time and effort by parking their lunch wagons permanently in the neighborhoods near the factories. They removed the wheels and converted their wagons into diners. In an effort to attract customers who wanted to sit down to eat their meals, they installed a row of fixed stools in front of a counter. Some enterprising business people even bought used street trolleys or railroad cars and converted them into diners. During the later part of the nineteenth century, diners were so popular and profitable that they could be found in virtually every neighborhood in large cities throughout the United States.

While most diners did a good business, they did not enjoy a good reputation. They attracted customers not because the food was delicious, but because it was cheap, conveniently located, and required a minimum of waiting. Widespread suspicion grew that much of the food served by the diners was not really fit for human consumption. Most middle-class people would not think of eating at a diner.

At the beginning of the twentieth century there were three kinds of eating places in most U.S. cities: a few expensive, high-quality restaurants catering to the wealthy; scattered individually owned restaurants

Diner customers, like this truck driver at an establishment in Indiana around 1940, usually ate at a long counter seated on stools.

offering the ethnic foods common in their neighborhoods; and clusters of cheap, individually owned diners or lunch counters serving low-wage workers in the cities. Most Americans never went to any of these establishments.

In the course of just over a century, food service has changed beyond recognition. The number of eating establishments in the United States has mushroomed to more than 1 per every 1,000 people. Middle-class families, who seldom darkened the door of a restaurant in the past, have become the mainstay of many food-service establishments. Americans of all economic levels commonly go out to eat simply as a form of entertainment or because they do not feel like making the effort of preparing a meal at home.

Recent surveys have found that almost nine out of ten Americans eat out once a week. More than a third of the population visits a fast-food restaurant every day.

Not only has the food industry changed beyond recognition, but it has also changed the way Americans live. Food service has become so fast that people can pick up a meal within a minute or two of ordering it. This has eliminated the necessity of mealtime being a long break in the day when people are forced to stop or at least slow down from their normal bustle of activity. Now families can rush directly from work to a Little League baseball field, with only the brief interruption of picking up supper at a fast-food place.

The fast-food industry has also catered to the idea that convenience and saving time are worth the price of increased waste. The plastic and paper containers that the food industry introduced in its attempts to bring faster service have reinforced the "throw-away" mentality of modern society.

The change in food service has even altered the American landscape beyond recognition. As Joseph Monninger wrote in an article for *American Heritage*, "American towns are dominated, architecturally, and in terms of landscape, by fast-food outlets." No longer do cities offer a unique set of restaurants stamped with the character of the local culture and the individuals who started the business. Now the familiar, brightly colored logos of a few nationally marketed businesses greet visitors on the outskirts of major cities and in many smaller towns. A person cruising along one of these fast-food "strips" can hardly tell Miami from New York or Oklahoma City. Indeed, one can scarcely travel to any urban center in the world without seeing the golden arches of McDonald's.

This book introduces some of the innovators and business wizards who shaped the fast-food business into the giant, influential service industry that exists today. These entrepreneurs perfected franchise systems and french fries; they introduced new foods and faster ways to serve or deliver them. Perhaps most importantly, they succeeded because they figured out what people like. In the process, they changed the way many Americans—as well as others throughout the world—live and, well, eat.

In January 1990, a customer eats a hamburger at the grand opening of the first McDonald's restaurant in Moscow, Russia.

1

FRED HARVEY

HARVEY'S HOUSES BEGIN THE CHAIN RESTAURANT

"Go west, young man!" influential newspaper publisher Horace Greeley urged adventurous Americans in the mid-nineteenth century. He might have added, "Be sure you bring your own food."

In the years following the Civil War, the railroads brought thousands of settlers and travelers to the West, but decent meals were left behind. Hungry passengers encountered greasy dining shacks set up in towns along the railroad routes. Menus consisted of moldy bacon, stone-hard biscuits, unrecognizable stew, leathery meat, eggs preserved in lime, and a pot pie that one historian described as "upper and lower crusts of cardboard held together with thick glue."

"Service" was a word that had little meaning west of St. Louis. Those who sold what passed for meals

Englishman Fred Harvey (1835-1901) brought good food and the idea of the chain restaurant to the American West.

Newspaper publisher Horace Greeley (1811-1872)

George Mortimer Pullman (1831-1897) was a cabinet maker before he designed and began manufacturing the Pullman sleeping car in 1865. His dining car came three years later.

on the train route took advantage of their customers at every turn. One common trick was for a train depot restaurant to insist that customers pay in advance for their meal. Then, just as the meal was served, the engineer would sound the train bell, alerting passengers that their transportation was about to leave. Fearful of being stranded in this forsaken depot hundreds of miles from any real town, customers rushed for the train and left their dinners behind. Restaurant managers then reheated the meals and served them to the next batch of train passengers, or pulled the same trick on them. They shared their ill-gotten profits with the railroad engineers who were in on the scam.

The prospect of getting a decent meal on a western rail trip was so bleak that even the railroads advised passengers to carry their own lunches with them. This food often attracted a horde of flies to the cars for the duration of the trip.

George Pullman tried to solve the problem by building a small kitchen with folding tables in one of his sleeping cars. The idea seemed promising enough that he constructed his first dining car in 1868. But its menu was limited, and the dining atmosphere was cramped and uncomfortable.

WORKING HIS WAY FROM THE BOTTOM

The person who brought real food service to the American West was a prim and proper Englishman named Frederick Henry Harvey. Born in London in 1835, Fred immigrated to the United States at the age of 15. He started his restaurant career on the

lowest rung of the ladder, as a pot scrubber for the Smith and McNeill Cafe in New York City.

The thrifty Harvey saved enough money from his $2-per-week pay to sail to New Orleans a few years later. His experience at Smith and McNeill helped him land a position at one of the city's finer restaurants. Harvey again saved his money carefully in hopes of owning his own restaurant. After narrowly surviving an epidemic of yellow fever, he moved to St. Louis in 1857. On the edge of the

Train passengers in the 1800s brought their own food as well as cooking and eating utensils for the long journey west.

western frontier, St. Louis seemed like a favorable location for a poor but hard-working young man to establish himself. Still short of cash, Harvey found a business partner who helped him open a restaurant. He settled down with his 17-year-old bride, Barbara Sarah Mattas, into what he hoped was a stable, respectable life.

The restaurant struggled, however. Although he worked hard to attract customers, Harvey ran into one obstacle after another. The outbreak of the Civil War uprooted many St. Louis residents and brought lean times to most of the rest. A severe outbreak of typhoid fever ravaged the town, hurting business further. Harvey was one of many who caught the disease and was house-bound for several months. When he recovered enough to return to work, disaster awaited him. His partner had given up on the restaurant, salvaged what money he could from it, and left town.

HARVEY AND THE RAILROAD

With his savings and business gone, in 1862 Harvey had to take a job as a mail clerk with the railroads. He later advanced to become general freight agent for the Chicago, Burlington & Quincy Railroad. Harvey's job required riding the trains throughout the West, where he ran into the horrid eating and lodging conditions that all rail passengers had come to expect.

For a man who had prided himself on running a respectable restaurant with good food, a clean dining area, and polite service, the ordeal of meals in depot eating places was especially miserable. Harvey put up with it for a number of years, but in 1875, he could stand it no longer. Although burned badly by his previous experience operating a restaurant with a business partner, Harvey decided to try again with a different partner. He did not see how he could fail this time. The railroad was bringing a steady stream of customers. The competition was so pathetic that people would rush to the most modest restaurant like drowning swimmers to a lifeboat.

In the course of a few months, Fred Harvey opened two restaurants along a railroad route, one in Wallace, Kansas, and the other in Hugo, Colorado. Once again, though, he showed poor judgment in his choice of business partners. Thanks to his partner's negligence, the ventures floundered. But instead of being discouraged by another failure, Harvey set his sights even higher. He was absolutely certain that railroad passengers to the West were desperate for a reliable high-quality place to eat. If he could be the first to provide luxury dining that rivaled the best restaurants in the East, there was no telling how rich and famous he could become. The only problem was that he did not have the financial resources to get the project going.

This 1870 wood engraving pictured the accommodations offered by a restaurant and hotel along the Pacific Railroad line.

THE PERFECT PLAN

In 1876, Harvey hit upon the perfect partner for his plan: his employer. He saw that any rail line that could offer its passengers a great dining experience would enjoy a huge advantage over its competitors. He could help the Chicago, Burlington & Quincy

Railroad by giving them that advantage; the railroad could help him by providing support for the venture. All he had to do was convince his bosses.

The Burlington Railroad, however, did not find merit in the plan. Undaunted, Harvey approached a rival—the Atchison, Topeka and Santa Fe Railway. Charles Morse, an executive with that company, saw the potential in what Harvey proposed. The two struck a deal. Harvey would provide high-quality eating places with good food, reasonable prices, and efficient, courteous service at stops along the Atchison, Topeka and Santa Fe line. In exchange, the railroad company would deliver his supplies free of charge. Harvey and Morse closed the deal with a handshake. Despite his past experiences, Harvey insisted that a gentleman's word was sacred.

Harvey began his enterprise in a grubby 10-seat lunch counter at the company's Topeka, Kansas, depot. He cleaned it up, hired employees carefully, and trained them to give polite, efficient service. With the railroad providing free freight for him, Harvey could afford to bring in better food than any competing lunch rooms offered while charging customers reasonable prices.

Harvey's lunch counter had barely opened before it was so crowded with customers that he had to expand. Even local residents stopped in at his new restaurant to enjoy the good food, something unheard of in the West at that time. At the age of 41, Fred Harvey had finally established a successful restaurant.

Charles Adelbert Morse of the Atchison, Topeka and Santa Fe Railway

An Outrageous Gamble

The triumph seemed to go to his head. Harvey began making an outlandish plan to open a world-class restaurant in the middle of nowhere. He bought a small hotel in Florence, Kansas, a town with a population of fewer than 1,400 people, and totally remodeled it. He brought in expensive furniture and crystal from England and ordered the finest china from France. His most daring move of all was hiring Konrad Allgaier, head chef at the famous Palmer House in Chicago, for $5,000 a year

The Harvey lunch counter at the Emporia, Kansas, station

(an incredible salary at the time) to move to Florence and prepare the meals. Allgaier bought products from local farmers and ranchers and paid them so well that they competed with each other to see who could provide him with the best-quality food.

To the astonishment of almost everyone, Harvey's gamble paid off. As he had predicted, his special treatment from the Atchison, Topeka and Santa Fe helped the railroad as much as it helped him. His restaurant was such a novelty and drew such rave notice from customers that many travelers to the West made a point of arranging their plans to include a dinner stop at Florence.

HARVEY HOUSES

Encouraged by his success, Harvey moved on to the next stage of his plan—a chain of "Harvey House" restaurants. By 1883, he had established 17 such restaurants scattered along thousands of miles of the Atchison, Topeka and Santa Fe line. His empire had grown so big that he resigned from his job as freight agent to devote full time to managing his chain from an office in Leavenworth, Kansas.

Harvey spent little money on the actual buildings in which he placed his restaurants. For example, the Harvey House in Holbrook, Arizona, was nothing more than a couple of old railroad boxcars joined together and spruced up. But once customers walked in the doors, they found the eating atmosphere the equal of many fine restaurants in big cities. The dining room was spotlessly clean. The tables for eight were elegantly set with polished silver and exquisite china. His managers knew that they had better arrange their tables with care. If Harvey arrived on a surprise visit and found a table was not set to his standards, he would yank the tablecloth, causing dishes and utensils to crash to the floor.

Instead of the basic, unappealing menu of stew and biscuits found at most railroad depots, Harvey House customers could order such rare delicacies as blue point lobster salad, roast sirloin, baked veal, or fresh whitefish from the Great Lakes—all transported in the railroad's ice cars. Fresh fruit, pastries, and ice cream were typical of the special treats Harvey could offer. Whereas other railroad depots served bitter coffee made with brackish local water, Harvey's customers enjoyed coffee brewed with pure, fresh water brought in by railroad tank car. Orange juice was always freshly squeezed. Some food critics proclaimed the fare at the Harvey Houses to be the best in the land.

Although Harvey's standards for food, service, and atmosphere were high, he kept prices low enough for virtually all travelers to afford. During most of the 1880s, all meals in the dining room cost 50 cents. Customers could order the same food for even less if they ate at the lunch counter. In 1888, the price for a dinner went up to 75 cents, 50 cents at the counter.

Unlike most rail depot dining operators of the time, Harvey went to great lengths to provide the best possible service for his customers. Realizing that tight train schedules made passengers anxious about finishing their meals before having to board again, he worked with the railroad to develop an ingenious system. The train conductor would ask the passengers whether they preferred to eat at the lunch counter or the dining room. Sometimes, he would even give them a choice of menu items. At the last stop before the Harvey House, the conductor would wire ahead with the number of customers and their dining choices. When the train was a mile from the restaurant, the engineer would toot the horn to warn the manager. When the passengers sat down to eat, the tables were set and the first course was on its way from the kitchen.

These passengers debarking at the Emporia, Kansas, station were expected and welcomed at the local Harvey House.

Service at a Harvey House was as impressive as the food, thanks to Harvey's demanding standards. Once while visiting his Harvey House in Raton, New Mexico, Harvey was appalled by the rude, sloppily dressed waiters and fired them all on the spot. The incident led him to believe that he could maintain a more civilized dining atmosphere if he hired only young women as servers.

Since few young women traveled through or lived in the West at that time, Harvey had to recruit help in the East. He put ads in eastern newspapers seeking attractive, intelligent women from 18 to 30 years of age. The wages he offered, $17.50 per month plus tips and room and board, were far higher than most working women could earn at that time. By offering so much, Harvey could afford to be choosy. While casual with his own business deals, he insisted that his waitresses sign a contract in which they swore to their good character, agreed to work at least a year, and promised not to marry during that time. (Later, contracts were for six- or nine-month periods.) The women were expected to work hard for their wages, putting in 12-hour days, six or seven days a week.

Determined to reinforce the concept that Harvey Houses were wholesome eating establishments and not the bawdy saloons for which the West was known, Harvey dressed his waitresses in long black skirts and white aprons. He had them live in company-owned dormitories under the strict eye of matrons who rigidly enforced a code of conduct and a 10 P.M. curfew six days a week. Anyone who missed three curfews could be fired. The code also protected the reputations of the young women during a time when women were discouraged from working and waitressing was considered one of the lowliest occupations.

The Harvey House waitresses turned out to be the best publicity move Harvey ever made. The "Harvey Girls," as they became known, attracted national attention. Many young men in the West visited Harvey Houses in hopes of finding a Harvey Girl to marry.

The famous humorist Will Rogers once referred to Fred Harvey as the man who "has kept the West in food and wives."

A CIVILIZED ATMOSPHERE

Having gone to great lengths to provide a refined, high-class dining experience, Harvey was not about to let any unruly customers spoil it for the others. In the "Wild West" of the 1880s, this was a difficult and sometimes dangerous challenge. Yet even in towns famous for lawlessness, such as Dodge City, Kansas, and Las Vegas, New Mexico, Harvey enforced strict rules. He insisted that all men wear jackets in the dining room. All customers were expected to behave properly.

In 1883, a band of drunken cowboys rode into Las Vegas, New Mexico, with their guns blazing. Laughing and shouting profanity, they barged into the barroom of the Harvey House hotel and began shooting at the bottles of liquor behind the bar. Fred Harvey happened to be visiting at the time and, without hesitation, confronted them. "Gentlemen,

ladies are here," he said, coolly. "No swearing or foul language is permitted. You must put up your guns and leave quietly at once." Caught off guard by the Englishman's scolding, the cowboys sheepishly returned their guns to their holsters. Harvey treated them to a meal (with lots of black coffee) in the dining room—after they donned jackets, of course.

The well-appointed Harvey House dining room in Bisonte, Kansas, about 1926

KEEPING AN EYE ON THE EMPIRE

The Harvey Houses proved so profitable for the Atchison, Topeka and Santa Fe Railway that the company renewed its deal with Harvey in 1889. Harvey won the exclusive right to operate all eating houses along the rail line. The railroad agreed to provide not only free delivery of food, fuel, ice, water, and restaurant supplies, but also free transportation for Harvey House employees. When the railroad added dining cars to its operations four years later, it awarded Harvey the contract.

As his chain of Harvey Houses continued to grow, Fred Harvey traveled constantly in search of the best sources of food and supplies. To ensure that all of his restaurants maintained the same high quality, he

Advertising was among the many sound business strategies started by Fred Harvey. This pamphlet for travelers described the meals and prices and assured passengers they would have ample time to enjoy their food.

standardized some of his operations. The Harvey Houses were given similar floor plans and interior decorations, and were operated under similar rules. Harvey then hired quality control inspectors to travel to the various restaurants and report on what they found. These inspectors had the power to fire managers who violated Harvey's rules of conduct.

RISE & FALL OF THE EMPIRE

Fred Harvey was never content to rest on his achievements. He kept dreaming up ways to expand his empire. By the beginning of the twentieth century, he had built luxury hotels and had added gift shops to many of his restaurants. These shops featured Native American crafts from the Southwest, such as rugs and pottery. When his health began to fail in late 1900, Harvey turned over a business empire of 47 restaurants, 30 dining cars, 15 hotels, and a huge Native American arts and crafts collection to his sons and son-in-law. He died a few months later, on February 9, 1901.

The Harvey heirs carried on the family tradition. At the chain's peak during World War I, more than 65 Harvey Houses prospered from Chicago to Galveston, Texas, and across the Southwest. But as travelers abandoned the railroads in favor of automobiles and airplanes, the Harvey Houses lost much of their business. Restaurant competitors in booming cities such as Los Angeles also cut into sales.

After a period of slow decline, business bounced back during World War II as hundreds of thousands of soldiers traveled the trains along the Harvey

The thousands of sailors and soldiers traveling by train during World War II gave the Harvey Houses a temporary boost of business.

House routes on their way to training camps and assignments. In 1943, Harvey Houses served more than 30 million meals, recapturing the company's position as the largest restaurant chain in the world.

But the war provided only a temporary boost. With the building of the interstate highway system and the improvements made in air travel during the 1950s, rail passenger traffic all but died. The historic Harvey Houses vanished in the 1960s. Today, the Fred Harvey Company survives only as a small business operating resorts in Arizona, California, and Hawaii.

LEGACY

Fred Harvey is often remembered as an influential figure in the development of the southwestern United States. But Harvey was also a pioneer of the fast-food industry. He was the first to tap into the anxiety of travelers who were leery of the eating choices offered them in strange towns. His success with the world's first chain of restaurants over a wide territory demonstrated that customers will flock to a familiar restaurant of proven quality.

At a time when restaurants either catered to the wealthiest of society or served cheap meals to those who could not afford better, Fred Harvey was also the first to recognize the huge market for reasonably priced good food. He started out by earning a reputation for top-quality food, excellent service, an inviting atmosphere, and reasonable prices. He built on that good reputation by establishing new restaurants with the same name, service, and prices. He went to great lengths to provide efficient service in his hiring and training of employees. Finally, he developed a system of inspections to ensure that each restaurant would uphold the reputation of all Harvey Houses.

These are the very steps that modern fast-food chains follow to this day. Although the Harvey Houses opened before the era of fast food and the company never joined the trend that started in the 1920s, Fred Harvey had laid down a solid foundation on which fast-food entrepreneurs would build their new industry.

2

BILLY INGRAM & WALTER ANDERSON

WHITE CASTLE MAKES THE HAMBURGER POPULAR

No food has so drastically changed eating habits in the United States as the humble hamburger. Like the history of many foods, the origin of the hamburger is cloaked in mystery. No one knows when the first cook experimented with ground meat and bread and came up with the hand-held meal so popular today.

The word "hamburger" is an obvious reference to the German city of Hamburg. Yet the citizens of that community never tasted what we refer to as hamburgers until American food companies began selling them. The city was famous for a popular way of preparing pounded beefsteak that became

Partners Walter Anderson and Billy Ingram proudly display their first corporate airplane in 1927. Pilot Anderson loved to fly, but the planes also proved a practical way for the two businessmen to monitor their many White Castle restaurants.

known as "Hamburg-style steak." This item was included on the menu at Delmonico's restaurant in New York as early as 1834. The term apparently evolved into a catch-all for a wide variety of relatively inexpensive dishes involving pounded beef.

Today's hamburgers are made of ground, not pounded, beef. Ground beef probably first appeared in the form of meatballs. Grinding the meat was a way to make the cheaper and less desirable parts of the cow more appealing. When meat was ground, it was difficult to tell exactly what was in it. For this reason, the public suspected, probably with reason in many cases, that butchers were putting poor quality and even spoiled meat in their grinders.

Boosters in several cities have laid claim to the origin of the ground meat patty sandwiched between two slices of bread that has become today's hamburger. Some insist that Charlie Nagreen of Seymour, Wisconsin, served the first hamburger in 1885 at a county fair. Others argue that Louis Lassen, proprietor of Louis' Lunch, a restaurant in New Haven, Connecticut, was the first to make a hamburger in 1900. Still others, citing scant proof other than the name of the town, tout Hamburg, New York, as the hamburger's birthplace.

The earliest documented reference to a ground meat patty dates back to 1904 when a Texan named Fletcher Davis attracted publicity by selling onion-covered hamburger sandwiches at the St. Louis World's Fair. Most likely, sandwiches resembling today's hamburgers developed independently in a number of kitchens throughout the country at about this time. But while the origin of the hamburger lies shrouded in mystery, the men who established it as a mainstay of American diets are well known.

THE DRIFTER

J. Walter Anderson was born on a farm near St. Marys, Kansas, in 1880. His parents were hard-working Swedish immigrants who saved up enough money for their son to attend a college in Sedalia, Missouri. Walt transferred to Baker University in Baldwin City, Kansas, but to his parents' disappointment, he never finished college. After freezing for a semester or two in an unheated house, he left the university and began wandering around the midwestern plains. When he needed money, he found a job as a dishwasher or a cook.

Concerned that Walt was wasting his life, in 1905 his father bought a restaurant in Marquette, a small town in central Kansas, and gave it to his son to operate. Walt Anderson's effort at settling down lasted less than a year. Lured by the enchantment of the stage, he sold the place to finance a traveling show complete with his own orchestra. But his show business career lasted exactly three weeks.

The failure of the show sent him drifting back onto the plains, supporting himself with low-paying kitchen jobs. After a stint in Topeka, Kansas, he went out to Nevada and Utah, cooking for the railroads. Anderson returned to Kansas in 1912, where he continued to shuffle around from one low-wage job to another.

THE 5-CENT HAMBURGER JOINT

While working as a cook in a small Wichita, Kansas, cafe, Anderson experimented with grilled meat. He tried molding ground beef into different shapes and flavoring it with a variety of sauces and spices. He also found that the meat cooked faster on the grill if he pressed it flat with his spatula. Anderson's customers were especially fond of this flattened meat patty topped with onions. They preferred the patty served between two halves of a bun rather than between slices of bread.

For the first time in his life, Anderson was struck with a flash of business ambition. Why not start his own restaurant and sell this novel type of hamburger sandwich? Unfortunately, his years of drifting had left him with little savings and the banks were leery of lending money to a small-time cook who had trouble holding a job.

In 1916, though, he was able to borrow just enough to buy an old shoe repair stand. It was a tiny place, with barely enough room for three stools at the serving counter and a griddle behind it. Anderson could not even afford to purchase the food supplies he needed to get started. He was able to open only because a grocer loaned him five pounds of beef and a supply of buns on the promise that Anderson would pay him at noon from his morning's profit. Anderson charged five cents per sandwich and by noontime he had collected enough nickels to repay the grocer and purchase another supply of meat.

The cramped quarters actually proved a blessing for Anderson because they forced him to grill directly in front of his customers. At the time, many people suspected hamburgers were made of tainted meat. As tasty and affordable as Anderson's hamburgers were, customers were reluctant to be caught eating them. According to Anderson, "Mothers were ashamed to drive up in front of my dinky place and would park their cars around the corner and send their lads after the sandwiches." So Anderson also ground his meat openly in view of the customers, proving that he had nothing to hide. His exceptionally clean kitchen further boosted customers' confidence.

Word that Anderson sold tasty, affordable meals spread quickly throughout the working-class people of Wichita. Cashing in on his growing reputation, Anderson set up two more hamburger stands in different areas of the city over the next three years. Each was distinguished by its clean, attractive counters, and the sign advertising "Hamburgers 5¢." The sandwiches were too small—only about 1.5 ounces—to be considered a meal by themselves. Anderson encouraged customers to "buy 'em by the sack." The citizens of Wichita did. By 1920, Anderson was a respected, well-to-do businessman.

Still riding the popularity of his hamburgers, Anderson tried to lease a property owned by a dentist for yet another hamburger stand. To negotiate the deal, he turned to Billy Ingram, the real estate agent through whom he had bought his house.

Although his hamburger stands were not yet called White Castle, in 1920 Anderson was already using the slogan "buy 'em by the sack" to promote his product.

Ingram Moves In

Edgar Waldo "Billy" Ingram was the same age as Anderson, having been born in 1880 in Leadville, Colorado. His father, Charles W. Ingram, had bounced between jobs as government clerk, rancher, and railroad worker before buying a laundry in St. Joseph, Missouri.

Billy worked at the laundry during his high school years. Then he moved to Omaha, where he worked as a livestock reporter and editor for the *Omaha Bee*. Later, he moved over to the *Omaha Excelsior*, a smaller paper that gave him greater responsibilities. In addition to his reporting and editing duties, Ingram had to keep the financial books and sell ads. This whet his appetite for the business world, and in 1905, he joined the financial firm of R. C. Dun (later to become Dun & Bradstreet) as a travel agent. Two years later, the company transferred him to Wichita.

Bitten by the urge to be his own boss, Ingram left R. C. Dun and started his own real estate and insurance company. A sound businessman, he steadily built his business over the course of 13 years. Among his real estate clients was Walter Anderson, who in 1920 asked him to handle the lease he was trying to arrange.

Despite Anderson's success, people continued to think of hamburger stand operators as shady, fly-by-night characters. The dentist with whom Ingram was negotiating would not complete the deal unless Anderson obtained backing from a respectable source. The more Billy Ingram looked at Anderson's bustling operation, the more impressed he was. He offered to cosign the lease himself, providing the dentist with the security he sought. In fact, the more he thought about it, the better the opportunity seemed. Anderson had created a product that the public loved. Why not get in on the action? Anderson, who was never much interested in business dealings, agreed to take on Ingram as his partner.

Ingram sold his interest in the insurance and real estate business to his former partner and went to work full time on this new venture. Many in the Wichita business community were stunned that a man with a successful firm would leave it all to become involved in hamburger stands. But once Ingram made the decision, he never looked back.

WHITE CASTLE

As he analyzed this new business, Ingram saw that two almost opposite trends posed a threat to its success. First, the hamburger continued to suffer from an unsavory reputation. One prominent food critic advised his readers, "Beyond all doubt, the garbage can is where the chopped meat sold by most butchers belongs, as well as a large percentage of all the hamburger that goes into sandwiches." This lingering distrust limited hamburger customers primarily to working-class people. Yet while some turned up their nose at this food, Anderson's hamburgers became so popular with his customers that competitors cropped up on street corners throughout Wichita.

Billy Ingram (1880-1966) saw the potential in Walter Anderson's hamburger stands and seized the opportunity to become part of the business.

Ingram was determined to create a new positive image for hamburgers, starting with a new name for the company. He wanted a name that presented an image of cleanliness and purity. At the same time, the name needed to project strength and stability to combat the public suspicion of hamburger stands as quick-buck schemes.

Ingram settled on "White Castle" and used the castle theme to distinguish the business from competitors. Hamburger stands would not only sport the White Castle name, they would also look like castles—gleaming white castles, complete with turrets.

Although fourth in Anderson and Ingram's new chain of White Castles, number four was the first restaurant built to look like a castle. It opened on Douglas Avenue in Wichita, Kansas, in 1921.

CHANGING MINDS WITH HIGH STANDARDS

To further combat the greasy, unsanitary reputation of hamburger joints, Ingram issued strict rules about cleanliness and food quality. Every inch of every store and all utensils were washed each day. Ingram created high standards for employees, including hand-washing regulations, a health examination by a physician, and a dress code, and he took every opportunity to inform the public of these standards.

He scored a major victory in his quest to reassure customers about the quality of White Castle food when Wichita's most trusted meat packer, Arnold Brother's Meat Company, agreed to supply its ground beef. The high-quality meat was delivered fresh two to four times each day. Fresh buns also arrived at each store at least twice a day.

Ingram realized that if he wanted to expand the business, he would have to find a way to keep every store in line with those standards. One poorly run store could jeopardize all of his efforts to win customer confidence. The easiest way to ensure quality was to set up a system in which every White Castle was the same.

From the beginning, Ingram standardized all operations. Every new restaurant had the same layout, with five stools at a counter overlooking the grill. Ingram kept the menus as simple as possible for easier supervision. Each store served the same items: hamburgers, coffee, Coca-Cola, and pie. Only young men—ages 18 through 24—were hired and they all went through the same two-week training program.

"The day of the dirty, greasy hamburger is past . . . for a new system has arisen, the 'White Castle System.'"
—Billy Ingram

In 1886, John S. Pemberton mixed a syrup made of sugar and extract from kola nuts. An Atlanta druggist and soda-fountain operator combined Pemberton's new syrup with soda water, and the result was Coca-Cola. This refreshing, tasty drink that could be easily made from a concentrated syrup and stored without refrigeration won eager acceptance throughout the country. Pepsi-Cola, the brainchild of North Carolina pharmacist Caleb D. Bradham, quickly followed.

A typical White Castle restaurant complete with stools, grill behind the counter, an all-male staff, and everything shiny clean

In order to attract and keep top employees, Billy Ingram offered generous salaries and provided benefits beyond those of anyone else in the food industry. He had employees' uniforms and aprons washed free of charge. White Castle was one of the first businesses in the United States to provide a fund to help its employees pay for large medical expenses. This evolved into full medical insurance coverage for full-time employees and their families. White Castle was also one of the first to offer employees a profit-sharing system and cash bonuses for outstanding work.

Ingram also recognized a trend that would shape the food business for the rest of the century. The pace of life was accelerating. The traditional leisurely noon meal was fading from the scene as more people moved to the cities to work in factories, shops, and offices. They did not have time to return home for a meal or to eat in a full-service restaurant. Ingram declared that "a revelation in the eating business has come. Instead of having to go to a restaurant and wait half an hour for the noon lunch, one may step into a nearby hamburger establishment and partake in a hot, juicy hamburger, prepared instantaneously."

GALLOPING SUCCESS

Ingram's brilliant business decisions, combined with Anderson's superior product, made White Castle a quick success. By the end of 1921, the company had eight thriving outlets in downtown Wichita. The next step was to expand into other cities, where the White Castle reputation was not yet known.

For his first probe outside Wichita, Ingram selected El Dorado, Kansas, a small city about 30 miles northeast of Wichita. The two El Dorado White Castles became so profitable that within two years they attracted an offer that Ingram could not refuse. While willing to sell the stores, however, he was not willing to give the new owners the rights to the White Castle name.

In late 1923, Ingram made another expansion move, this time into Omaha. White Castle hamburgers proved so popular that he opened eight additional restaurants in Nebraska's largest city by the end of 1924.

White Castle grew at a galloping rate throughout the decade. Every few months, Ingram would set up White Castles in a new city, locating them in the industrial areas where he could attract the factory and shop workers who took to hamburgers so enthusiastically. Before 1924 was over, White Castle had moved into Kansas City, Missouri. The next year, the company opened the first of 18 restaurants in the St. Louis, Missouri, area. They expanded north to Minneapolis-St. Paul, Minnesota, where 20 restaurants were operating by the end of 1926. In these few locations, White Castle almost single-handedly changed the eating habits of the average worker. In 1925, White Castle served over 84,000 hamburgers, a food that had been virtually unknown a decade earlier.

COPYCATS

The tremendous success of White Castle attracted a host of competitors eager to cash in on this new market. Many competitors shamelessly stole every detail of the White Castle formula. They copied the name, the menu, and even the castle architecture. On street corners throughout the Midwest, hamburger restaurants bearing names such as White Knight Nickel Sandwich, Royal Castle, and Little Kastle sprang up. Some even brazenly advertised themselves as White Castle.

"Many historians point to the 1920s as the time when American culture as we know it today began. This was when many Americans bought their first automobile, their first radio, or voted in their first election. And yes, it was when most Americans tasted their first hamburger."
—David Gerard Hogan, *Selling 'Em By the Sack: White Castle and the Creation of American Food*

Major food-service chains showed no more regard for White Castle's trademark. In 1926, a chain of White Tower restaurants began in Milwaukee, Wisconsin. Riding the wave created by White Castle, White Tower for a time enjoyed even more spectacular growth than its rival. The Toledo-based White Huts followed, along with Tennessee's Krystal hamburger chain of 300 restaurants in the South. The flurry of imitators confused customers. Ingram fought hard in the courts to stop the worst offenders, with some success. After long legal battles, courts in both Minnesota (1930) and Michigan (1934) declared that White Tower had intentionally used the White Castle trademark, products, and methods to mislead the public and ruled in favor of White Castle.

GOING NATIONAL

At the close of the 1920s, some food experts continued to dismiss White Castle hamburgers as a peculiar taste of the Midwest. That theory was proved wrong when Ingram established successful White Castles in New York City in 1930. Sales of White Castle hamburgers topped the 21 million mark nationwide that year. Although he operated in only 12 selected cities, Ingram had clearly established the hamburger as a preferred meal of the urban work force.

Many ambitious owners in Ingram's place might have tried to take advantage of White Castle's raging success by quickly establishing restaurants in every sizable city across the country. But Ingram was a

Established in 1921 — HAMBURGERS — "Buy 'em by the Sack"

Compliments of Opening Crew #1-31

Bill Sang - Harvey Mock - Bob Butler - Vic Prince - Geo. Herrick

Opening day for Chicago's first White Castle restaurant in 1929. Chicago quickly became one of the company's most profitable areas.

conservative businessman. Debt made him nervous and he did not like sharing control of his company with others. Because of this, he set up a policy that has remained in place to this day: White Castle would build no new store until they had the cash in hand to pay for it.

Nonetheless, White Castle steadily spread into working-class neighborhoods of the country's big cities. In every new expansion, Ingram started by recruiting good managers and workers and training them in the company operations. He and Anderson regularly visited all of the cities in which their restaurants operated to see that they were being run properly. Anderson's love of flying prompted White Castle to be among the first corporations to use air travel to keep tabs on business. These inspection tours were Anderson's main contribution to the company during the partnership—he was happy to let Ingram handle the rest. But his folksy style and daring air trips, recounted faithfully in the company's newsletter, made him so popular with White Castle managers and workers that when Ingram bought out Anderson's shares in the company in 1933, the sale was not announced for two years.

DEPRESSION AND WAR

As the business grew, Ingram found it increasingly difficult to maintain standards of quality in each of his far-flung restaurants. Rather than relying on suppliers to provide the food and other materials that his company required, he decided to produce the supplies himself.

The Paperlynen Company opened in Green Bay, Wisconsin, in 1932 to produce paper hats and aprons. Ingram had wanted to reduce laundry costs while maintaining cleanliness, and the paper products accomplished this goal. He also set up the Porcelain Steel Building Company to manufacture the white steel enamel panels out of which the White Castle restaurants were constructed. Kitchen fixtures and griddles were also made from this easy-to-clean material. Both divisions relocated to Columbus,

Among Billy Ingram's many business innovations was the company newsletter he started, *Hot Hamburger* (later renamed *The White Castle Official House Organ*). Ingram wanted to promote uniformity and create camaraderie among his workers. Employees and even customers sent in contributions and eagerly awaited each month's issue. Described in the newsletter, Walter Anderson's aviation exploits captivated readers.

51

Workers fabricate the turrets used to construct White Castle restaurants at the Porcelain Steel Building factory in Columbus.

Ohio, in 1934 when Ingram moved the company headquarters there from Wichita to be more centrally located among the 130 White Castle restaurants. Both divisions profitably made products for other companies as well.

Through Ingram's leadership, White Castle continued to grow during the Depression years of the 1930s, a time when many companies failed. The company served more than 40 million hamburgers in 1937, almost twice the 1930 figure. The number of employees also doubled, from 300 to 600, between the years 1929 and 1935.

Commodity restrictions and a severe labor shortage during World War II were more difficult for Billy Ingram to deal with. The military needed the same young men White Castle preferred to employ, so for the first time women were hired. The restaurants dealt with shortages of sugar, Coca-Cola, coffee, meat, and even ketchup. Some stores no longer operated 24 hours a day. With many supplies that restaurants needed to stay in business unavailable, to remain profitable White Castle reduced the number of its restaurants.

In an effort to increase sales and dispel the impression that White Castle restaurants were patronized mainly by working-class men, the company hired a corporate hostess during the Great Depression years. Using the name Julia Joyce, she visited women's clubs and organizations and introduced hamburgers to middle-class women, some of whom did become new customers.

Although the public liked White Castle hamburgers as they were, Ingram kept looking for ways to improve them. Cincinnati operator Earl Howell noticed that putting five evenly spaced holes in the patty helped it cook faster and improved the taste. This method also used 10 percent less meat, important to the company as shortages continued and price controls went into effect during the Korean War (1950-1953).

Billy Ingram retired in 1958 at the age of 80. His son, Edgar, took over the company. At that time, White Castle served more hamburgers than any other restaurant chain in the world. But lifestyle changes in the United States during the 1960s toppled the company from its lofty perch. The mass migration of Americans to the suburbs left White Castle's inner-city restaurants in a bad position. With their stools and counters, these stores were geared to walk-in business, not the drive-in business that would soon dominate the fast-food industry. White Castle's policy of refusing to franchise restaurants or to borrow money to finance expansion also hindered the family-owned company from matching the rapid pace set by McDonald's and others. Nonetheless, the company continued to grow slowly and remain profitable after 1960.

Today, White Castle enjoys a mystique fed by its fanatically loyal customers. People who live far from the nearest White Castle have been known to order the hamburgers packed in dry ice and shipped to them by overnight express. Legendary singer Frank Sinatra had them shipped to his concerts. Such loyalty keeps the company among the top ten hamburger restaurants in the United States, even though it no longer holds a dominant position in the fast-food industry.

LEGACY

Billy Ingram followed in the path of Fred Harvey by building a chain of restaurants with an emphasis on cleanliness, quality food, and reasonable prices. Like Harvey, he was able to offer customers predictability. People who walked into a White Castle restaurant knew exactly what they would get. Ingram carried this concept of restaurant standardization a few steps further. Today's large fast-food chains have learned from him that the easiest way to guarantee a high level of quality in a vast, far-flung enterprise is to have the individual stores be as similar as possible.

The little square hamburger that changed the way Americans eat

More importantly, fast food could not have grown into the multi-billion-dollar industry it is today without the introduction of new food products. Perhaps hamburgers would have emerged as a favorite food in the United States without White Castle. Perhaps the fast-food industry would have mushroomed as it has without hamburgers. But the fact remains that Anderson and Ingram achieved the feat of taking the little-known and poorly regarded hamburger and making it acceptable, even desirable. The company then led the expansion that marketed this product—now considered a symbol of modern American culture and cuisine—across the world.

3

J. F. McCullough & Harry Axene

THE KINGS OF DAIRY QUEEN

Almost every child and adult alive in America today has had the pleasurable experience of licking off the curl on top of a Dairy Queen ice cream cone. Since 1940, people of all ages have been lining up on warm summer evenings to purchase something cold and sweet from Dairy Queen.

The company enjoyed explosive growth after World War II, spreading quickly across the country into thousands of neighborhoods in small towns as well as big cities. Today, some Dairy Queens offer meals in addition to cones, shakes, sundaes, bars, and splits. But the menus still revolve around the unique soft ice cream. So who invented this ice cream? And how did outlets serving it spread so far so fast?

Customers lined up to taste the soft ice cream made by J. F. "Grandpa" McCullough (1871-1963).

GRANDPA MCCULLOUGH'S IDEA

J. F. McCullough, known to his friends and family as "Grandpa" McCullough, began selling ice cream in 1927, when he was 56 years old. A few years later, he and his son Alex decided to go into business manufacturing their own product. They bought an old, wood-frame cheese factory in Green River, a small town in northwestern Illinois, and converted it to an ice cream plant. McCullough moved into a building across the street so that he could keep a close eye on the operation.

Over the next few years, the McCulloughs collected milk from local farmers and turned it into ice cream under the Homemade Ice Cream Company label. The ice cream initially had to be soft—at 23 degrees Fahrenheit—so that it would pour out the spigot of the ice cream freezer into the three-gallon tubs that were sold to retailers. After that, it had to be frozen to a solid -10°F so that it could be stored and transported more easily. J. F. McCullough noticed that the soft ice cream that poured into the containers tasted better than the finished frozen product. The ice cream was frozen for the convenience of the maker and seller, but McCullough thought it was a shame not to give customers the best-tasting ice cream he could make.

Curious to see if his instincts were right, he proposed an experiment to one of his retail customers, Sherb Noble. McCullough would bring some five-gallon tubs of soft ice cream to Noble's Kankakee, Illinois, store for a special sale. Since the soft ice cream would not keep for long, they needed a catchy promotion that would bring in a steady stream of customers. On August 4, 1938, they posted a sign outside the store that read, "All the Ice Cream You Can Eat for Only 10 Cents." As Noble later commented, "We attracted a crowd that almost pushed our front window in." The crowd loved the ice cream. Noble and his workers frantically dipped soft ice cream into 16-ounce cups—1,600 servings in two hours—until the tubs were empty.

FINDING A MACHINE

The customers' response had reinforced Grandpa McCullough's belief that the flavor of soft ice cream was better. But he could not rush tubs of soft ice cream every day of the year to every store that sold his products. He needed a machine that could make a continuous flow of soft ice cream right at the store. Unfortunately, there was no such thing, and the two equipment manufacturers Alex McCullough contacted expressed no interest in making one.

The next year Alex did a double take when he was driving through Chicago's southeast side. There was a frozen-custard stand advertising "ice cream frozen the second before you eat it." This was the very thing the McCulloughs had been looking for. Alex stopped, looked at the equipment, and asked the operator for the name of the person who had made it. But the man refused to give out the information.

Frustrated, Grandpa pored over want ads from the *Chicago Tribune*. A few days later, he found what he was looking for: a small advertisement for a

Sherb Noble was the first to serve the new soft ice cream at his store in Kankakee, Illinois.

continuous ice cream freezer/dispenser. Grandpa arranged a meeting with the advertiser, whose name was Harry M. Oltz. They worked out a contract that gave the McCulloughs the right to manufacture Oltz's patented machine as well as exclusive rights to use it in Illinois, Wisconsin, and all states west of the Mississippi River. In exchange, Oltz would receive a royalty of a few cents per every gallon of ice cream made with his machines.

Although Oltz's machine produced the soft-serve ice cream they desired, the McCulloughs found that it still was not practical for a small ice cream store. It

"Wouldn't it be great," mused Grandpa McCullough, "if there were a freezer that could dispense semifrozen ice cream that still held its shape?" Harry Oltz's first freezer, below, accomplished that.

was big, clunky, and difficult to operate. Two people had to haul tons of ice and salt up a ladder and pour it in the top of the freezer. The only way they could tell if the ice cream was the correct consistency was to see the finished product, and the only way to see inside was to attach a mirror that could be viewed from the top of the ladder. The McCulloughs also found that the salt, as well as detergents used for cleaning, quickly corroded the metal.

Working in Grandpa McCullough's basement, Alex and the company's first employee, Herb Klavohn, tinkered with Oltz's invention through the

The Homemade Ice Cream Company's first employee was Herb Klavohn (right), shown here inspecting an ice cream machine with his son Francis.

winter of 1939-40 to make it suit their manufacturing needs. While they did so, Grandpa ran batches of ice cream mix through the freezer to find the process that produced the best ice cream. Visitors occasionally found ice cream mix splattered over the walls from a test run that went haywire. Through trial and error, Grandpa found that a butterfat mix of 5 to 6 percent (lower than that used in standard ice cream) worked best with soft serve and that 18°F was the ideal temperature. Once they got the machine in good working order, the McCulloughs arranged with Stoelting Brothers, a dairy equipment manufacturer in Kiel, Wisconsin, to build the new five-foot-long freezers for them.

QUEEN OF CREAM

Grandpa McCullough and Sherb Noble set up a store in Joliet, Illinois, to test their new product. Grandpa named the store "Dairy Queen" because he believed his soft serve was the best, a "queen" among dairy products. The store opened on June 22, 1940, selling soft serve in cones, sundaes, pints, and quarts.

The machines were still far from perfect. They were bulky, and the chain belt drive on the auger that mixed the ingredients was so loud that the store managers had trouble hearing the customers' orders. But the new soft-serve product quickly won enthusiastic fans. In its first summer, the store paid back all the money the McCulloughs and Noble had invested in it. In 1941, the McCulloughs built a second Dairy Queen, in Moline, Illinois. As soon as it opened, a line formed that stretched clear around the block.

Dairy Queen was so successful that business people constantly approached McCullough, asking for a piece of the business. By this time, Howard Johnson's had demonstrated the potential of franchising food services. Fearing that soft-serve ice cream might be just a short-term fad, however, the McCulloughs did not try to build their own chain. Instead, they began charging a one-time fee to individuals for the right to operate Dairy Queens in different territories.

The first Dairy Queen store opened in Joliet, Illinois. Owned by Sherb Noble, it was managed by Jim and Grace Elliott.

Harry and Wanda Axene pictured with their son Norman (center) in 1942

World War II put a damper on expansion because the U.S. government rationed the sugar needed for Dairy Queen mix and the materials necessary to manufacture new freezers. But by 1943, five Dairy Queen stores were up and running in Illinois, with queries for more arriving steadily.

AXENE WANTS IN

It was then that Harry W. Axene and his wife, Wanda, drove by the East Moline Dairy Queen. Born in Moline in 1905, Axene had joined his father and three brothers as a farm equipment salesman. In 1943, he was working as sales manager for the St. Louis branch of the Allis Chalmers Company. But with metal being diverted to the war effort, Axene's company cut production, leaving Axene with few new machines to sell. So he frequently visited his family in Moline.

While driving into town, Axene noticed long lines forming at the window of what appeared to be a store. Curious as to what product could attract such crowds, he stopped to investigate. He found the soft-serve ice cream to be delicious. Like many people, he wondered if there were a way for him to get into this thriving business.

Harry's brother Everett happened to be a good friend of the Dairy Queen manager, Jim Elliott, so he introduced the two. Elliott directed Harry to see Grandpa McCullough about the possibility of obtaining a Dairy Queen franchise.

Axene drove to Green River, where he found Grandpa McCullough sitting on his front porch. It so happened that 72-year-old McCullough was ready to retire. He was an ice cream maker, not a business executive, and the growing responsibilities of licensing Dairy Queen were tiring. Taking an immediate liking to the big, friendly salesman, McCullough offered Axene half ownership of his ice cream mix company, as well as the rights to operate Dairy Queens in Iowa and Illinois, for $12,000. When Axene admitted he had only $5,000, McCullough accepted that as a down payment. Although Grandpa McCullough would live another 20 years with his daughter, Esther, in Davenport, Iowa, he had little involvement in the business once he sold out to Harry Axene.

Making a clean break from his Allis Chalmers job, Axene bought McCullough's house across the street from the mix plant and went to work. He and Wanda lived in two rooms plus the kitchen and used the rest of the space as a business office.

The cone with the curl on top

THE MEETING

Harry Axene hoped to build Dairy Queen through a franchising strategy. Unlike McCullough, he was a businessman who had some idea of how to do it, and his timing was perfect. With the end of World War II in 1945, many former soldiers returned to the business world and were looking for small investment opportunities.

Axene hit the jackpot when one of his suppliers, the Illinois Cone Company, tipped him off to a list of investors who had an interest in the ice cream trade.

Summoning all 26 investors to a meeting at the LeClaire Hotel in Moline, Axene brought out charts and graphs showing them what they could expect to earn from a Dairy Queen franchise. He offered to sell each of them a territory in which they would have exclusive rights to operate Dairy Queens. The operators would also have to pay him a royalty on the soft serve they sold, ranging from 19 cents to 34 cents per gallon, depending on how much they paid him up front. A master salesman, Axene finished his presentation by bringing in samples of the soft-serve ice cream to share with the prospects.

In a flurry of wheeling and dealing, Axene amassed a fortune. Alex McCullough, who retained the other half of the business, was selling franchises, too. Sometimes, rather than charging a royalty on each gallon of ice cream made, McCullough and Axene accepted a one-time payment. Eager franchisees paid as much as $100,000 for exclusive Dairy Queen rights to a large territory.

Axene's idea triggered an explosion of Dairy Queens across the nation. Before his meeting with the 26 investors, there were a total of 8 Dairy Queens in operation. Two years later, more than 100 stores were cranking out ice cream so fast that Stoelting Brothers could not keep up with the demand for freezers. They contracted with a second supplier. A year later, in 1948, the Dairy Queen chain swelled to 400 stores and it passed the 1,400 mark two years after that. Within a decade of its birth, Dairy Queen had grown into the largest and most widespread food-service franchise system in the world.

GROWING PAINS

Harry Axene was breaking new ground in his explosive expansion of Dairy Queen and so it was not surprising that he made some mistakes. While he raked in money hand over fist, he had no plan for the quality control and formal organization that White Castle and Howard Johnson's had considered crucial. Franchisees were free to operate their stores any way they wished. In the words of one owner, "Dairy Queen started by growing arms and legs all over the place, but it was a body without a head."

Franchisees organized the Dairy Queen National Trade Association in 1948 to try to take advantage of the franchise system. But their efforts were not always successful. Each Dairy Queen added its own limited menu of food to complement the ice cream, and these independent operations proved expensive. They could not join together to purchase supplies in bulk, which would have greatly reduced their costs. Nor could they join together to pay for a national advertising campaign. As a result, the quality varied greatly from restaurant to restaurant.

Axene began to lose interest in Dairy Queen after selling territorial rights in California to family friend George Foster. During a trip out west in 1947 to help Foster open his first store, Axene decided he had had enough of Illinois winters. He moved to La Jolla, California, and his brother Clarence took over the ice cream mix plant in Green River. Having sold off all his Dairy Queen territories, Axene had no reason to stay with Dairy Queen and left a year later.

Not only did Harry Axene sever his ties to Dairy Queen, but he also went on to organize its greatest competitor. In 1949, he joined with Leo Maranz, an inventor who had designed a smaller, more efficient soft-serve freezer, to form the Tastee Freez company. While the company quickly spawned 600 franchises, Maranz and Axene did not see eye to eye on business matters. Within two years they dissolved their partnership. Axene hung on to his Tastee Freez franchise rights on the West Coast until his retirement in 1981. He died in 1988.

Howard Johnson & The Franchise

When people think of fast food, Howard Johnson's is not a name that normally comes to mind. Howard Deering Johnson (1896-1972), however, claims a place in the history of fast food because he perfected the idea of restaurant franchises.

A franchise is a licensing arrangement in which an investor pays money to the owner of a particular brand-name product or business for permission to sell that product or operate that business in a certain territory. The person offering the permission is called the franchiser. The person buying the rights is the franchisee.

The idea of franchising dates back to the time of the Civil War in the United States. The Singer Sewing Machine Company, established by Isaac Singer in 1858, needed a factory that could mass produce its sewing machines. In order to raise the money, Singer sold the rights to market his machine to local business people and trained them in its use. From the fees he collected, Singer was able to finance the expansion that has made the company a respected name for over 140 years.

No significant business followed Singer's lead until, around the turn of the century, the Coca-Cola company sold the rights to bottle and distribute its soft drink to a number of individuals. By 1921, Coca-Cola boasted a network of more than 2,000 bottlers and had increased nationwide sales.

In 1919, Roy Allen bought a small, walk-up root beer stand in Lodi, California. The

Known as the "host of the highways," Howard Johnson's restaurants offered take-out, counter, or dining service. Children were welcomed with highchairs and child-size portions and prices.

root beer recipe he used won raves from customers and attracted a business partner, Frank Wright, who joined Allen in 1922. Taking the initials of their last names, Allen and Wright renamed their business A & W.

Instead of following Coca-Cola's lead and selling bottling rights to A & W root beer, Allen and Wright grew their company by selling the rights to operate root beer stands bearing the A & W name. They continued to profit by selling their root beer concentrate to their franchisees. By the time Howard Johnson began franchising his restaurants, A & W root beer stands were popping up in many western states.

In 1925, Johnson borrowed $500 to buy a run-down drugstore with a soda fountain. He began experimenting with ice cream recipes high in butterfat content, cranking out gallon after gallon of different flavors. After he replaced the soda fountain's commercial ice cream with his own home-made flavors, business took off. Johnson then began setting up small ice cream stands on the beaches around Boston. This idea proved so popular that he sold 14,000 ice cream cones on a single hot summer day. Encouraged by his success, Howard Johnson decided to open restaurants that would serve meals as well as ice cream.

Building a business during the Great Depression years of the early 1930s was difficult. Learning from his mistakes and taking on a dangerous amount of new debt, he built a string of 25 restaurants along Massachusetts highways, splashing the roofs with distinctive orange paint so that customers would instantly recognize the buildings. He featured the ice cream for which he was known.

In 1935, Reginald Sprague, a friend who owned land along the highway near Cape Cod, tried to interest Johnson in leasing the land for yet another restaurant. Johnson agreed that the location was good. But his expansion had put him too deeply into debt for him even to consider the offer. He made a counteroffer. If Sprague would put up the money for a restaurant, Johnson would let him use the Howard Johnson name and products. Johnson would train whomever Sprague hired in the operation of the restaurant. Sprague agreed, creating the nation's first restaurant franchise.

Chains of restaurants had existed before this time. The early operators of eating houses took advantage of their good reputation to set up other restaurants of the same name in different locations. A chain of restaurants, however, is different from restaurant franchises. Harvey House and White Castle were restaurant chains, owned by the company, not by independent operators.

Howard Johnson's first restaurant franchise turned out to be more successful than he dreamed. Both he and Sprague made a handsome profit. Johnson saw at once that franchises were the way to go. The Howard Johnson name was so respected among customers in New England that it drew far more patrons than a new restaurant could have attracted on its own. With little investment from Johnson, his name was spreading farther and farther across the east. At the same time, he was building up an ever larger base of restaurants to which he could sell his products. By 1941, more than 150 orange-roofed Howard Johnson restaurants dotted the East from Maine to Florida. When Johnson began adding hotels next to his restaurants in the 1950s, there were 400 Howard Johnson outlets along the nation's highways.

Although Howard Johnson's restaurants were never considered fast food and their influence in the food industry has faded, the company blazed the franchise path followed by many fast-food companies ever since.

Among those gathered for the first Dairy Queen National Trade Association meeting was Ray Kroc, facing the camera and seated beside a woman at the left end of the front table. A supplier at the time, Kroc later formed a corporation to franchise McDonald's restaurants.

GETTING ORGANIZED

Following the departure of Axene, and then the retirement of Alex McCullough in 1953, growth of the loosely organized Dairy Queen empire slowed. In the 1950s, supermarkets began offering inexpensive ice cream that took away much of Dairy Queen's take-home market. The growing popularity of television as well as the rising number of air-conditioned buildings and homes made people less likely to go out for an ice cream treat.

Operators responded by offering more products and food. Malts and shakes had been introduced in 1949; banana splits arrived in 1951. Sundaes with a variety of toppings and the popular Dilly Bar appeared in the mid-1950s. Through these efforts, Dairy Queen did manage to double the number of its stores to 3,000 by 1960.

Then in 1962, a group of territory operators provided structure to the Dairy Queen system by banding together to form International Dairy Queen (IDQ). They purchased the national and international franchise rights from Hugh McCullough, who had taken over his family's interests in the business when his father, Alex, retired. The corporation also bought back many territories from franchisees, and launched the chain's first national advertising program. Gil Stein became the first president of the new company, which located in Minneapolis.

A Dairy Queen sundae

That same year, IDQ adopted the Brazier hot-food menu as the official food system for those Dairy Queens that offered items in addition to ice cream. James Cruikshank, an operator in Georgia, developed the system because he wanted the stores to operate year-round—many were open only in the summer—and he believed the food should be uniform in each outlet. The name "Brazier" came from his idea to charbroil the hamburgers on a grill.

DECADES OF GROWTH

International Dairy Queen enjoyed dramatic growth during the 1970s and 1980s. By 1980, the company's 4,833 stores passed the $1 billion mark in sales. This volume placed Dairy Queen fifth in the fast-food industry, behind only McDonald's, Kentucky Fried Chicken, Burger King, and Wendy's.

In 1985, one of the company's most popular products was launched—the Blizzard, an extra-thick shake flavored with fruit or candy or cookie bits. IDQ sold 100 million Blizzard flavor treats the first year this product was on the menu, with figures rising steadily since. The company continued to grow by acquiring two smaller franchisers, Karmelkorn in 1986 and Orange Julius in 1987. The Berkshire Hathaway Corporation in Omaha assumed control of IDQ in 1998, by which time nearly 5,800 Dairy Queen outlets were serving customers in the United States and Canada.

Iowa Dairy Queen operator Ron Medd developed the popular Blizzard treats and the special mixer required to make them.

LEGACY

Food industry analysts credit Dairy Queen, particularly Harry Axene, with creating the fast-food franchising system as we know it today. He showed

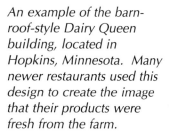

An example of the barn-roof-style Dairy Queen building, located in Hopkins, Minnesota. Many newer restaurants used this design to create the image that their products were fresh from the farm.

how a businessperson could make a mind-boggling profit from selling the territorial rights to use a single piece of food manufacturing equipment and a recognized brand name. Dairy Queen's growth—from a single store in 1940 to more than 1,400 just one decade later—fanned the flames of the franchise revolution that others had started.

Dairy Queen successfully targeted small towns, the only food chain to do so other than A&W. The company continues to be successful, however, because of the unique treats based on the soft ice cream developed by Grandpa and Alex McCullough. "At Dairy Queen," wrote John A. Jakle & Keith A. Sculle in *Fast Food*, "it is what comes after the hamburger that counts."

4

THE McDONALD BROTHERS

THEY PUT THE "FAST" INTO FAST FOOD

Neighbors of Maurice and Richard McDonald would have seen a bizarre sight had they looked out their windows late one night in 1953. The brothers had asked the entire night crew of their restaurant to come to their home in San Bernardino, California. There the workers shuffled around the tennis court, pretending to flip hamburgers, fill cups with soda pop, and serve customers, while the McDonalds scrambled around them, drawing red chalk lines on the cement to indicate where kitchen equipment should be placed.

The exercise was one of the McDonalds' creative attempts to design the most efficient restaurant

The McDonald brothers, Richard (1909-1998, left) and Maurice (1902-1971) did almost everything together, including finding the fastest way to flip burgers.

kitchen imaginable. Although an unexpected morning rain shower washed out the chalk marks before a draftsman could copy them onto paper, the brothers' obsession with speed and efficiency did pay off in the end. Not only did they make their restaurant hugely profitable, but they also threw the entire fast-food industry into a new gear.

MAC AND DICK HEAD WEST

Maurice McDonald and his younger brother, Richard, better known as Mac and Dick, were raised in Bedford, New Hampshire. Their comfortable world was shaken when the shoe factory where their father worked as foreman was forced to close during the Great Depression. Not wanting to trust their fate to an employer who could lay them off in a flash, the young men decided to go into business for themselves. In 1930, equipped with high school diplomas and a desire to succeed, the brothers headed across the continent to California, hoping to find a better economic climate.

The McDonalds started out as stage hands for a Hollywood motion picture studio while they scouted the business possibilities. They found what they were looking for—a movie theater in the Los Angeles suburb of Glendale. Running a movie theater, however, proved unprofitable. Despite the generous help of the landlord from whom they rented the theater, the brothers struggled for four years. In all that time, they never made enough to even pay the full monthly rent on the building.

Looking around for a more promising business opportunity, they considered a California craze: the drive-in restaurant. California culture of the 1930s was centered almost entirely on the automobile, and restaurants there responded accordingly. They surrounded their stores with large parking lots that served as dining areas. The restaurant buildings served as kitchens. Waiters and waitresses, known as carhops, worked outdoors, relaying orders from customers and carrying out the food. Many restaurants experimented with special features designed to appeal to motorists. Some installed speaker phones that allowed customers to place an order directly from their cars. Others tried gimmicks such as carhops on roller skates.

This was the business the McDonalds chose to enter in 1937. They started serving hot dogs and shakes from a small stand near Pasadena. The brothers served the walk-in customers who sat on a dozen stools outside the order window, while three carhops handled the parking lot business. Responding to suggestions from their customers, they gradually switched from hot dogs to hamburgers.

The stand brought in considerably more money than the brothers' theater venture, but they saw potential for even more. In 1940, they built a larger store in San Bernardino, a growing working-class town 50 miles east of Los Angeles. Dick, who had a knack for marketing, designed an eye-catching octagonal building with windows that slanted in

Drive-Ins: Catering to Motorists

When the Pig Stand opened along a busy Dallas, Texas, highway in September 1921, the drive-in restaurant was born. J. G. Kirby came up with the idea of a restaurant where customers could drive into his parking lot and order a hot barbecued pork sandwich without ever leaving the car. By 1934, there were 100 Pig Stands selling "America's Motor Lunch" in Texas, California, New York, and several southern states. Cooking barbecue was labor intensive, however, and the chain declined after World War II.

But the drive-in restaurant lived on. The automobile had become an important factor in the food-service industry as more people came to rely on it for virtually all their transportation needs. As early as 1924, Roy Allen and Frank Wright included drive-ins among their chain of A & W root beer stands in the western United States. In the 1930s, the success of Howard Johnson's showed that a restaurant chain could make a fortune appealing to hungry motorists.

It was not until the 1940s that fast-food drive-ins roared ahead of inner city walk-in stands such as White Castle. Hamburger drive-in restaurants with carhop service were popular into the 1950s. In the effort to speed service and save on salaries, most drive-ins later switched to window service.

Drive-through dining is a more recent innovation. Customers read the offerings from an outside menu, speak to restaurant employees through a microphone, then pick up and pay for their orders at a window, all without ever leaving their cars. Dave Thomas, founder of Wendy's restaurants, is credited with popularizing this innovation.

To compete with other hamburger chains, White Castle offered carhop service at some outlets between 1936 and 1972.

toward the roof. Like their previous stand, the new McDonald's restaurant had no indoor seating. While they provided a few stools next to the counter, the McDonald brothers took direct aim at the drive-in business. Their parking lot could accommodate as many as 125 cars, and they hired 20 carhops, all young women, to serve these drive-in customers. The menu featured 25 items, including hamburgers, beef and pork sandwiches, and barbecued ribs.

The McDonalds' focus on motorists paid off. By the mid-1940s, business was steady. San Bernardino construction crews and other wage-earners lined up

The original McDonald's restaurant in San Bernardino, California, pictured in 1948

for a quick, satisfying lunch. At night, cars full of teenagers ordered meals while using the parking lot as a gathering spot. The restaurant cleared $50,000 per year, enough for the brothers to buy a 25-room house on a hill and engage in their one splurge— trading in for a new Cadillac every year.

STARTING FROM SCRATCH

Instead of enjoying their success, the McDonald brothers grew bored with it. They had few interests outside their business, with the exception of boxing, and the restaurant had ceased to be challenging. As Dick explained, "The money was coming in, and there wasn't much for us to do."

But then in 1948, with new drive-ins springing up all over the greater Los Angeles area, the McDonald brothers took a hard look at their restaurant and saw some things that disturbed them. McDonald's had become known as the city's teen hangout. While that was good for teens, the brothers saw it as bad for business. Many customers, particularly families, avoided the place at night when the teens took over. The brothers began to worry that the competition would squeeze them out of business if they could not expand their market beyond the teen crowd.

The McDonalds had also grown irritated with the carhop situation. They were constantly hiring new ones to replace those who quit after only a few months or even weeks. Carhop service was an expensive and slow method of serving food. Customers eating in their cars created a crowded, noisy environment. Some of the silverware taken out to the cars never came back, and broken dishes were also eating into profits. At one point they decided to sell the restaurant and open a different one in a new shopping center. But fear of the unknown overcame them. They knew they could run a drive-in. Why risk their future on some new gamble? At the last minute they decided to search for new challenges in the drive-in business.

After discussing the situation, the McDonalds decided they would be better off without the carhops. They would still cater to motorists, but the motorists would park in the lot and walk up to the window for service. Obviously, if they were going to ask customers to give up the service they had come to expect, they needed to offer something in its place to keep them satisfied. The McDonalds decided to start over from scratch and concentrate on offering the three things most important to a drive-in customer: good food, low prices, and fast service.

To the astonishment of customers and competitors alike, the McDonalds fired all their carhops. "The carhops were slow," remembered Dick McDonald. "Customers weren't demanding it, but our intuition told us that they would like speed." So they closed their doors for three months in the fall of 1948 while they overhauled their entire operation. They analyzed every part of their restaurant in an effort to cut costs and speed up the service. After studying their sales receipts, they discovered that 80 percent of their customers ordered hamburgers. So they scrapped the expensive barbecue sandwiches, tore out the old three-foot grill, and replaced it with two six-foot grills so they could cook hamburgers by the dozens. At a time when most fast-food restaurants such as Dairy Queen and A & W were adding menu items, McDonald's cut offerings from 25 choices down to 9: cheeseburgers, hamburgers, three soft drinks, milk, coffee, potato chips, and pie. They dressed all burgers the same way—with ketchup, mustard, onions, and two pickles—rather than adding condiments according to each customer's order. They further cut costs and increased service speed by using paper bags, wrappers, and cups, thus eliminating plates, silverware, and the need for a dishwasher.

Having reduced service and menu options, the McDonalds had to come up with a spectacular deal to lure customers. So they slashed the price of the hamburgers from 30 cents to 15. Although they also trimmed the burgers from one-eighth to one-tenth of a pound, the price cut was an enormous risk. Despite drastically lowering their operating costs, making a profit from 15-cent hamburgers would require a large number of customers.

DISASTER TO TRIUMPH

The new McDonald's got off to a terrible start. Customers blared their horns, angrily waiting for carhops to serve them. They hated the change and many of them took their business elsewhere. Rather than increasing sales, the new "Speedee Service System" lost nearly 80 percent of the restaurant's business.

But the brothers stubbornly stayed with their new format, the only change being the addition of milkshakes and, one year later, french fries. Within six months, the restaurant began to recover. New customers loved the low prices and appreciated the fast service. Just as the McDonalds had hoped, the elimination of carhops ended the restaurant's appeal as a teen hangout. That business was replaced by parents thrilled that they could treat the entire family to a restaurant meal at a reasonable price, with no waiting.

The McDonald brothers demonstrate their Speedee Service System.

Children liked the food and enjoyed being able to place their own orders at the walk-up window. Recognizing that they had tapped into a whole new market for food service, the McDonalds focused their advertising on families.

By the end of 1949, long lines were forming at the order windows. McDonald's attracted so many customers that, even with their Speedee Service System, the McDonald brothers kept searching for ways to speed up production. They began making shakes and frying hamburgers in advance of the noon and supper crowds. The shakes were stored in a refrigerator, and the hamburgers were packaged and placed under heat lamps to keep them warm. The

The McDonald brothers discovered they could create more business by offering less—fewer menu choices at lower prices.

McDonald's Speedee Service

MENU

HAMBURGERS	15¢
CHEESEBURGERS	19¢
MALT SHAKES	20¢
FRENCH FRIES	10¢
ORANGE	10¢
ROOT BEER	10¢
COFFEE	10¢
COKE	10¢
MILK	10¢

brothers invented their own tools and utensils, such as a 24-bun lazy Susan that speeded up the preparation of burgers. They coaxed their suppliers into devising new equipment, such as a one-squirt ketchup dispenser.

The McDonalds made a scientific study of their operation. They broke down the preparation of a hamburger into simple, repeatable steps. Instead of hiring experienced cooks who were each responsible for preparing a hamburger from start to finish, they hired untrained workers (men only at first) and gave each a specialized task. In effect, they turned the kitchen into an assembly line that enabled them to serve customers almost immediately even at the busiest times.

Over the next two years, customers swarmed to McDonald's restaurant in San Bernardino. Word spread quickly throughout the country of the Speedee Service System that was daily satisfying thousands of customers. In 1951, annual sales reached $277,000, up 40 percent from the carhop days. *American Restaurant Magazine* featured McDonald's in its July 1952 issue. Curious restaurant owners called the McDonald brothers, begging to know how they managed their operation.

BIRTH OF THE GOLDEN ARCHES

Realizing they had designed a system that could revolutionize the restaurant business, the McDonalds began to entertain the idea of licensing their Speedee Service System. In 1952, they worked out an agreement with Neil Fox, a gas-station owner who wanted

Taco Bell Rings In

Glen W. Bell Jr. was a telephone repairman who regularly ate lunch at the McDonald's in San Bernardino when it first opened up. After seeing the tremendous business that the McDonald brothers' new Speedee System was attracting, he decided to go into the fast-food business himself. In 1952, he persuaded a friend who worked as a contractor to build him a restaurant patterned after McDonald's.

In addition to hamburgers, though, Bell added tacos to the menu. Tacos were one of the foods that Mexican migrant workers had brought with them when they traveled through California. Over the years, some of the migrants had set up open air stands to sell their food to those who had developed a taste for it. While the competition among hamburger restaurants was fierce, no one else had tapped into the growing market for Mexican food. In 1962, Bell dropped hamburgers from the menu and put his own name on his stores along with his main product. The result was Taco Bell.

By 1975, Bell had franchised 673 units. Three years later, PepsiCo bought Taco Bell and added drive-throughs and slick advertising to boost business. The strategy worked. In 1990, there were 3,500 restaurants and this figure would double by the end of the decade. In 1997, PepsiCo created a subsidiary company called Tricon Global Restaurants to run Taco Bell as well as the other two restaurant chains it owned, Kentucky Fried Chicken and Pizza Hut.

to start a restaurant in Phoenix, Arizona, patterned after McDonald's. For the modest fee of $1,000, the McDonalds agreed to provide Fox with a plan of their kitchen layout, a manual describing the Speedee Service System, and a week of training. To the brothers' surprise, Neil Fox asked if he could use the McDonald's name as well. Although they could not understand why he would want to use a name that meant nothing to the people of Phoenix, the McDonalds agreed. By this time the brothers had thought of new ways to improve their kitchen efficiency. As part of their agreement with Fox, they let him use the new, much larger store design that they were working on.

The McDonald brothers hired a local architect to render their ideas for a flashy red-and-white tiled roof that slanted sharply from the front to the rear. But when Dick McDonald saw the finished plans, he was disappointed. The building looked too flat, too ordinary. McDonald wanted a more distinctive look, something like the turrets used on White Castle outlets or Howard Johnson's orange roofs, which would set McDonald's apart from competitors. While pondering the problem, he scribbled some arches on a sheet of paper. Unfortunately, according to McDonald, his architect thought the arches were "terrible" and refused to add them.

Too stubborn to give up on his idea, Dick McDonald brought his concern to George Dexter of the Dexter Sign Company. Dexter told McDonald to let the architect finish the plans minus the arches. When the building was finished, he would cut holes in the roof and add them. Accustomed to using bright colors in his signs, Dexter suggested arches painted a brilliant yellow.

AS BIG AS THEY WANTED

Over the next two years, the McDonalds sold 15 franchises without much effort. Although not all of those who bought franchises opened restaurants, the brothers' profits still doubled to more than $100,000 per year. But they had neither the desire nor the training to transform their enterprise into a large corporate organization. Neither cared to travel and

Dick (seated) and Mac McDonald (right) review plans for a new, larger restaurant.

they absolutely refused to fly, which made them totally uninterested in going around supervising franchises. Instead of protecting their trade secrets and pocketing millions of dollars dividing the country into franchising territories, they showed their operation to anyone who asked. Some of the people to whom they gave tours went home and copied everything they saw without paying a dime for it.

Soon competitors were springing up all over California, luring away McDonald's customers with the brothers' own system. The McDonalds, however, were not particularly concerned. As Dick explained, "We couldn't spend all the money we were making. We were taking it easier and having a lot of fun doing what we wanted to do."

When one of their suppliers, Ray Kroc, offered to franchise the McDonald's system in 1954, the brothers were happy to let him do it. In December 1961, Kroc bought all rights to use and license the McDonald's name. The brothers dropped out of the restaurant scene, leaving only their name behind.

LEGACY

Mac and Dick McDonald were the ones who put the "fast" in fast food. Once they established a system that could provide almost instant hot meals, other restaurants had to follow their lead in order to compete. Carhops disappeared from roadside restaurants, replaced by self-service counters. When McDonald's replaced the experienced short order cook with an assembly line that cranked out hamburger after identical hamburger, the entire drive-in industry went to automation. The McDonalds showed how to take unskilled workers and train them in a system that produced consistently high-quality food, allowing fast-food restaurants to replace cooks with young, inexperienced, low-wage workers. By the 1980s, more people would begin their experience in the work world at McDonald's than at any other company in the country.

McDonald's efficient system also dropped the price of a meal so low that, for the first time, even relatively low-income families were drawn into the restaurant market. The entry of this enormous segment of the population into the world of fast food changed not only the food industry, but also the way Americans eat.

Mac retired to Palm Springs, California, where he died in 1971. Dick returned to Bedford, New Hampshire, where he lived until his death in 1998—long enough to witness the phenomenal growth of the company he and his brother had founded. Asked years later if he had any regrets about selling their business, McDonald replied that he had none. "I would have wound up in some skyscraper somewhere with about four ulcers and eight tax attorneys to pay all my income tax," he said.

5

RAY KROC

SERVING BILLIONS AT McDONALD'S

In the summer of 1954, food-service equipment salesman Ray Kroc became intrigued with a restaurant named McDonald's that had purchased several of his Multimixers, an electrical appliance with five spindles that could mix five milkshakes at a time.

This was not the first time Kroc had heard mention of that California hamburger stand. His West Coast representative had been telling him about this remarkable fast-food place for over a year. Kroc had also seen an advertisement in a national publication seeking investors interested in owning a McDonald's franchise. Curiosity ate at him until he just had to travel to California and see for himself.

Although he had made an appointment with the McDonald brothers, who owned the restaurant, Kroc

Ray Kroc (1902-1984) saw the potential of a small drive-in called McDonald's and turned it into a huge multinational business.

first did some investigating on his own. He parked in the McDonald's lot at 11 A.M. and watched. He had barely turned off the ignition when customers began forming lines at the two front windows. By noon, he counted 150 people. To his amazement, one after another quickly departed with a bag of food. Kroc had never seen anyone serve hot food that quickly and to so many people. He talked to customers who all gave glowing testimonials about the food and service. After Ray Kroc met Dick and Mac McDonald, he made up his mind to get involved in the business somehow. He had no idea what a far-reaching decision he had just made.

One of Ray Kroc's Multimixers churns out milkshakes for McDonald's restaurant

Raymond Albert Kroc was born in Chicago on October 5, 1902, the eldest of Louis and Rose Kroc's three children. Even as a child, he preferred work over anything else. "I got as much pleasure out of work as I did from playing baseball," he remembered—and he loved baseball. During his younger days he ran a lemonade stand and later found jobs at a grocery store and drug store. While he was still in school, he started his own music shop with two of his friends.

At the end of his sophomore year of high school, the United States became involved in World War I. Ray enlisted in the Red Cross Ambulance Corps and completed his training in Connecticut. But the war ended just before he was to board a ship for France.

Ray returned home to Chicago, where he sold ribbon novelties and tried to establish himself as a piano player. In the summer of 1919, he joined a band in the resort town of Paw-Paw Lake, Michigan, where he met and began a romance with Ethel Fleming.

In 1920, the Western Union Telegraph Company transferred his father to New York, and Ray's family insisted that he go with them. While in the east, he worked for a stock brokerage firm, but the office closed after a year and he returned to Chicago—and Ethel. His father told him he could not marry until he had a full-time job. So in 1922, Ray Kroc found work as a salesman with the Lily Cup Company and won his father's approval to marry. He continued to pursue his musical dream as well, playing piano for a local radio station at night.

The paper cup business was slow at first, especially in the winter. So in late 1924, Kroc, his wife, and their baby daughter moved to Florida, where he sold real estate until the land boom there went bust. He fell back on his piano playing until 1926, when he returned to Chicago and the Lily Cup Company, having decided to devote his energy to sales.

THE CAREER SALESMAN

Ray Kroc spent the next 25 years selling paper products to the convenience food industry, which was still in its infancy. Along the way, he learned a great deal about his customers. Kroc had the knack of putting himself in their shoes and discovering what they really needed. He worked hard at finding ways to help his clients succeed by using his product, a strategy that also resulted in increased sales for him.

For example, in 1930 Kroc persuaded the purchasing manager of Walgreen Drug Stores to try expanding lunch-counter service to include carryout in just one of the Chicago stores. The new service was so profitable that Walgreen, the largest drugstore chain in the Midwest, added carryout in all of their stores, and the manager bought the paper containers needed for this new venture from Ray Kroc.

Kroc's alert scouting for new products and services for his customers led him into the ice milk business in the early 1930s. While on a sales call at an ice cream shop in Battle Creek, Michigan, his client showed him a new premixed ice product.

Consisting of stabilizers, corn syrup, and vanilla, the ice stirred up easily into a delicious milkshake and replaced the traditional, more expensive ice cream. Immediately, Kroc saw what this product could do for ice cream retailers he served in the Chicago area. He introduced the new product to Earl Prince, who ran a chain of ice cream stands. Prince quickly introduced the new milkshake. Both parties profited—the ice cream sellers from the popular, convenient product, and Kroc because more milkshakes meant he could sell more paper cups to the retailers.

THE MULTIMIXER MAN

In the late 1930s, Earl Prince and ice cream figured in a major career move for Ray Kroc. Prince had invented a milkshake mixer with one motor that drove five spindles capable of making five shakes at a time. Kroc knew that some of his ice cream retailers were having trouble keeping up with milkshake orders, especially on hot days. This Multimixer seemed the perfect answer. He tried to persuade the Lily Cup Company to distribute it, but to his frustration, Lily refused.

Kroc considered leaving his job at Lily. That scared his wife, Ethel. "You are risking your whole future if you do this, Ray," she warned him. But Kroc was so convinced that the Multimixer was a sure-fire money-maker that he decided to gamble and obtained the marketing rights to the device. He set up his own company, Prince Castle Sales.

Unfortunately, just as Kroc was building up his sales, World War II began. In order to preserve supplies for the military, the U.S. government banned the sale to civilians of copper wire—a crucial component of the electrical motor that powered the Multimixer. From 1942 until the end of the war in 1945, there were no electrical motors to put into the Multimixers.

Left without a product to sell, Kroc scrambled to survive. He struggled through the war years by taking advantage of another government restriction—sugar rationing. When ice cream retailers complained of a shortage of sugar for their milkshakes, Kroc stepped in by selling them a corn-syrup substitute.

When the war ended, Kroc again had Multimixers to sell. But the astounding growth of Dairy Queen restaurants in the 1940s plus the migration from the cities to the suburbs stole customers away from the drugstore soda fountains that were Kroc's best customers. By the early 1950s, soda fountains were in deep trouble and so was Ray Kroc. He had sold 9,000 Multimixers a year in the late 1940s, but now he had to work long hours just to peddle 2,000. The sales force he had carefully built up was wiped out. Kroc's only hope was that he could sell his Multimixers to the emerging fast-food restaurants.

A LATE CAREER CHANGE

By the time he met the McDonald brothers, 52-year-old Ray Kroc was in the late stages of a long and sometimes disappointing sales career. The last thing he had expected when he talked with Dick and Mac McDonald was to involve himself in a brand new

Ray Kroc demonstrating a Multimixer at a national restaurant show in 1957

enterprise. But Kroc had seen the birth of the fast-food franchise industry close up. Entrepreneurs could go into business and make money almost immediately. No wonder Big Boy restaurants, Dairy Queen, and others had been able to sell so many franchises.

Kroc thought that the same thing could happen with McDonald's restaurants. The brothers already had established a food preparation system that was far faster than any other restaurant's. All Kroc had to do was find investors and persuade them that a McDonald's franchise was the chance of a lifetime. It was a mission custom-made for a career salesman.

Influence of the Big Boy

Robert Wian was only 21 when he opened a hamburger joint in Glendale, California. One night members of a band that frequently ate at his place complained that a hamburger was not a real meal. In response, Wian served up two hamburger patties between three slices of bun garnished with mayonnaise, lettuce, cheese, and relish. The Big Boy, as Wian called it, became so popular that in 1937, Wian created a franchise chain named after it: Bob's Home of the Big Boy.

The franchise enjoyed great success for a number of years. By 1975, there were 103 Bob's Big Boys in southern California, and hundreds of others run by franchisees, such as Shoney's in the southeastern United States and Marc's in the upper midwest. Some restaurants were drive-ins, others offered more traditional sit-down dining.

Marriott Corporation purchased Bob's Big Boys and the franchise rights to the other restaurants in 1975. Marriott sold out to Elias Brothers, the Michigan franchisee, in 1988. A number of franchisees broke their association with Big Boy at this time.

Although no longer a force in the fast-food industry, in the late 1990s the chain still ranked third in size among family-style restaurants with 825 units. And the Big Boy hamburger—forerunner of such super-sized offerings as Burger King's Whopper and McDonald's Big Mac—remains at home on the menu.

The Big Boy still serves up the original double-patty burger at restaurants like this one in Essexville, Michigan.

Unlike many others who understood the value of what McDonald's was doing, Ray Kroc did not simply copy the McDonald's system and start his own enterprise. Throughout his career, he had been honest and open in his dealings. And initially he was not interested in running fast-food restaurants. All he wanted was to create a large new chain of clients for his Multimixer.

The more Kroc thought about it, though, the more he believed that this franchising opportunity had far more potential than increasing sales of the Multimixer. He decided to make McDonald's his main business. Within a week of meeting the McDonald brothers, Kroc offered to sign on as the brothers' national franchising agent. Franchising had never been a serious interest for the McDonalds, so the brothers accepted his offer. On March 2, 1955, Kroc formed his new franchising company, McDonald's System, Incorporated.

For six years, Mac and Dick McDonald continued to run their Bernardino restaurant while Kroc concentrated on establishing franchises. By December 1961, however, the brothers wanted to retire—and Kroc was ready to take over the whole business. He purchased all rights to the McDonald name and licenses for $2.7 million.

THE FRANCHISES COME FIRST

Although he had no training or experience in building a franchise chain, Kroc had a long career in sales that had taught him the secret of success. Whether selling to a one-person ice cream stand or a giant corporation such as Walgreen, Kroc had learned that his success depended on his customers' success.

From watching the saga of the Dairy Queen chain, Kroc believed that the same approach would work with other fast-food franchises. He had seen Dairy Queen's explosive growth and the enormous fortunes made by Harry Axene and other franchisers. But in recent years, Dairy Queen had begun to flounder because, Kroc believed, Axene and the others had not concerned themselves with the success of the franchises. By collecting an up-front fee for the franchises and, in some cases, charging them a stiff royalty percentage for the use of the soft-serve machines, they had saddled many of the stores with a crippling financial burden. Because they had made their fortunes early in the game, the Dairy Queen franchisers had little interest in seeing that the stores were profitable.

Kroc was determined not to make the same mistake. His first goal was to see that everyone who bought a McDonald's franchise would have a profitable restaurant for many years to come. In contrast to all other food franchises, Kroc arranged for the franchisee to make money before he himself did. He sacrificed his own comfort and security to keep the franchise fees low and the royalties paid on products to the bare minimum. For the first six years of his career with McDonald's, he never accepted a penny in salary, living instead off the modest income from his Multimixer sales. Even when his company ran into debt, he refused to squeeze his clients and employees. Instead, he borrowed against his own life insurance to make up the shortfall.

Ray Kroc wanted everyone in the McDonald's franchise to be on the same team. He wanted the franchisees to trust him just as if they were business partners. Therefore, unlike virtually all other food chains, he decided that McDonald's would not sell supplies to its operators. Instead, the franchises would join together to bargain for the best deal they could from suppliers.

Kroc also preferred to sell one franchise at a time. Franchisees had to prove successful before they were allowed to open more stores. Each McDonald's had to be operated in the same way, and each would have to pass standards for QSC: Quality, Service, and Cleanliness. V for value was later added to this McDonald's motto.

THE FRENCH FRY PROBLEM

Kroc wanted to build a showcase McDonald's that potential franchisees could visit. For his first restaurant, he chose a location in suburban Des Plaines, Illinois, that he admitted was unexceptional, but it was convenient to his home and office.

Immediately after opening the store on April 15, 1955, Kroc ran into a baffling problem with the french fries. Although the Des Plaines store made them exactly as the California McDonald's, the fries tasted "like mush." Convinced that the fries were a key factor in McDonald's success, Kroc frantically tried to find out what was wrong.

Ray Kroc's model McDonald's opened in Des Plaines, Illinois, in 1955.

After much investigation, he discovered that the cooler, wetter Midwestern climate was the problem. The desert air of San Bernardino had dried out the potatoes the McDonald's restaurant there used. This curing process was necessary to produce a potato that would fry up to the proper crispness. Kroc had a curing system designed. The potatoes were stored in the basement with a large electric fan blowing on them. So obsessed was Kroc with perfecting his fries that Ed MacLuckie, manager of the Des Plaines restaurant, commented, "We have the world's most pampered potatoes. I almost feel guilty about cooking them."

Ray Kroc went so far as to make a scientific study of potatoes. After determining the proper density of potatoes that produced the best fries, he told his suppliers that he would buy only potatoes that met his density guidelines. At first, the potato growers thought he was crazy. No one had ever paid any attention to potato density. Eventually, however, Kroc was able to order such huge quantities of potatoes that growers who wanted his business had to take him seriously.

Kroc's focus on quality control led to one of his company's most famous innovations: Hamburger University. Kroc set up the facility in 1961 in Elk Grove, Illinois, to ensure that all McDonald's operators would be well-trained to meet the standards Kroc had set and succeed as McDonald's franchisees. Hamburger U has grown from the basement of a McDonald's restaurant to its own building on the corporate campus in Oak Brook, Illinois.

French-fried potatoes first appeared on restaurant menus in the late 1890s.

McDonald's Takes Over

At the time Ray Kroc took control of McDonald's franchising, the fast-food company faced serious competition. White Castle was firmly entrenched in the cities. Meanwhile, new hamburger restaurant chains such as Burger King, Burger Chef, and Henry's were spreading throughout the country.

Many of them were touting the same type of fast service that the McDonald brothers had pioneered.

Kroc carefully nurtured his small chain of McDonald's franchises, some of which he sold to acquaintances who were neither wealthy nor experienced in the restaurant trade. He did whatever he could to keep them in business. In 1956, a total of 13 McDonald's were up and running in Illinois and

An early advertisement for McDonald's promoted "an all-American meal of a hamburger, a milkshake and french fries for only 45¢."

Indiana. By the end of the decade, Kroc had franchised more than 100 new restaurants.

Despite Kroc's success in the 1950s, McDonald's finished the decade as just one of many chains competing for the new fast-food dollar. In the 1960s, however, Kroc vaulted past them all. More than 1,000 McDonald's were in operation by the end of the 1960s. By 1974, this figure would reach 3,000.

Kroc's success came in part because he recognized the enormous appeal of fast food to families, a segment of the market that few restaurants courted. He also saw that the automobile had changed the way Americans lived. No longer did businesses and restaurants have to be concentrated in the cities, where mass transportation and high density population provided a large base of customers. Americans were coming to depend upon the automobile for almost all their transportation needs. Because of the easy mobility provided by cars, people were moving out to the suburbs where land was cheaper and neighborhoods quieter. Kroc followed these families out to the suburbs.

Ray Kroc flew across the country, scouting for new store locations. He zeroed in on middle-class communities, taking note of schools and churches that indicated a stable neighborhood. As fast as McDonald's made money, Kroc would sink the profits into inexpensive lots on the outskirts of these areas. By designing U-shaped parking lots, he avoided the need to buy more expensive corner lots that gas stations and other drive-up businesses demanded. McDonald's bought so much property that eventually it would own more land than any other corporation in the world.

Kroc was so successful in selecting locations for fast-food stores that others tried to ride on his coat-tails. As soon as word leaked that McDonald's had bought a piece of property, competitors rushed to purchase land nearby. The result was the birth of the fast-food "strips" that have come to dominate so many towns.

NEW PRODUCTS AND IDEAS

New products and creative advertising contributed to the remarkable growth of McDonald's during the 1960s. Although Ray Kroc knew little about advertising, he hired those who did. Then a pair of Washington, D.C., franchise operators enlarged McDonald's appeal to younger children by creating the Ronald McDonald clown character, and the company's advertising began to regularly feature Ronald.

Kroc looked to his employees and franchisees for new product ideas as well. Because he gave them the freedom to innovate, a steady stream of suggestions flowed into the company. In the early 1960s, a Cincinnati franchise operator introduced the Filet-O-Fish that now graces all McDonald's menus. The legendary Big Mac originated in 1968 with Jim Delligatti, who owned a dozen stores in Pittsburgh. Herb Peterson, an operator in Santa Barbara, California, introduced the Egg McMuffin in 1973.

During this growth time of the 1960s, the company went public, offering shares of stock for the

Two successful new food items that were tested and retested before being added to the menu: the Big Mac (above) and the Egg McMuffin.

first time. The price per share soared from $22.50 to $49 in just a few weeks after the initial offering in 1965. Ray Kroc was now a millionaire, as were two of his colleagues who had been with him from the beginning, June Martino and Harry Sonneborn. Going public also earned the company new respect in the business community. In 1985, McDonald's was added to the Dow Jones Industrials, a group of large companies whose daily stock prices are averaged to measure the movement of the stock market.

Kroc's personal life also took a turn for the better. He and Ethel had divorced in 1961, but then in 1969 he married organist Joan Smith, whom he called the "ideal partner in music and marriage." That same year he convinced his brother, Robert L. Kroc, to head up the Kroc Foundation. The foundation supports research in diabetes, arthritis, and multiple sclerosis. (Ray suffered from diabetes, as did his daughter.) Head of physiology at a large drug company, Robert was an ideal choice. Ray also spent part of his new fortune on some fun: in 1974, he bought the San Diego Padres baseball team.

LEGACY

Ray Kroc, who died in 1984, left a personal legacy as well as a financial one. A true salesman with a flair for dealing with people, he masterfully motivated his vast network of operators and suppliers. He won their loyalty by ensuring that they all became rich before he did. "Kroc's notion of a fair and balanced franchise partnership is without question his greatest legacy," said author John Love in *McDonald's: Behind the Arches*.

Furthermore, he ran this huge network so efficiently that McDonald's emerged as the clear-cut winner of the fierce competition among hamburger chains that began in the 1950s. Because of Kroc's efforts, McDonald's has long since passed the United States Army as the nation's largest training organization. As the world's largest purchaser of beef and potatoes, the corporation exercises a major influence over food producers throughout the world. McDonald's has established restaurants in virtually every major city around the world, selling more than $12 billion worth of food per year. The company's golden arches have become one of the most recognized symbols of modern American culture.

Modern McDonald's have increased in size and dramatically changed in design. Plentiful seating, playgrounds, and other family-oriented amenities give customers a relaxing place to eat a meal.

6

HARLAND SANDERS

DOING IT RIGHT AT
KENTUCKY FRIED CHICKEN

Colonel Harland Sanders gave a stock answer to those who questioned why he, well into his 80s, still traveled around the world promoting his Kentucky Fried Chicken. "A man will rust out before he wears out," he always said.

Sanders's strong work ethic and stubborn refusal to bow to the effects of aging created one of the most colorful stories in the history of fast food. For most of his life, he switched careers like a shopper trying on new clothes, looking for something that would satisfy his craving for attention. Not until after the age when most people retire did he find the success for which he had been searching. And in the process, he enticed people to include chicken on their list of fast-food favorites.

A gifted and innovative cook, Harland Sanders (1890-1980) also had a flair for promotion. These abilities helped him to make his chicken franchise a delicious success.

111

TOUGH CHILDHOOD

Harland David Sanders was born on a farm outside Henryville, Indiana, on September 9, 1890. His childhood ended abruptly at the age of five when his father, Wilbert Sanders, died. Margaret Ann Dunlevy Sanders leaned heavily on her young son as she struggled to provide for her family. At the age of seven, Harland took care of his younger brother and sister while his mother went off to work at a tomato canning factory. With some instruction from his mother and what he could remember watching her do in the kitchen, Harland had to learn to cook or else he and his siblings would go hungry.

Harland was free to attend school only in the winter. He did poorly in classes and finally dropped out altogether in the sixth grade. The summer he was 10, his mother packed him off to work on a nearby farm. But he did so little work that the farmer sent him home after a month. His disgusted mother exclaimed that he would never amount to anything. Ashamed, Harland determined to work hard from then on. The next summer he not only lasted the whole season as a farm hand, but was also invited to return the following year.

Problems continued on the home front, however. When Harland was 12, his mother married William Broaddu, a farmer in Greenwood, Indiana, who treated him badly. One night Broaddu beat Harland, so Harland's mother sent him to live with an uncle. His brother, Clarence, followed two days later, but Harland was already gone. His uncle had found him

Harland Sanders remembered one of his first cooking triumphs this way: "I . . . set the yeast, like [my mother] had done. Then I made the sponge, and mixed it and let it rise, got the oven hot, and put in the loaf. I kept watching it, and when I figured it was done, I took it out and let it cool. Then I gave Catherine and Clarence some. They said it was so good we ought to show it to Mama. So we took off . . . the dust on the road so thick it squirted up between our toes—we went barefoot in the summer, don't you see. We must have been a sight when we walked into the canning plant." All the women in the cannery tried a piece of Harland's bread and loved it, showering him with hugs and kisses. "I hated that," he said. "You know how little boys are."

a job as a farm hand. Two years later, his uncle helped him obtain work as a streetcar fare-collector. After a brief stint in the army, Harland Sanders became a deck hand on a river boat, and then landed a job as a railroad yard worker.

CURSE OF THE HOT TEMPER

At the railroad, Sanders showed signs of settling down. He became a fireman, shoveling coal into the engine that ran the train. He married Josephine King, with whom he had three children. Despite his lack of education, the ambitious Sanders took correspondence courses in law during this time. But his feisty nature continually caused him problems. After three years with the railroad, his outspoken union activities irritated management so much that they fired him. He found work with another railroad, only to get into a fight with an engineer that cost him the job.

Finding job opportunities was never a problem for Sanders and he took advantage of a train wreck to set himself up as a lawyer. Upon learning of the accident, he changed into a suit and rushed out to offer his services to those who were injured. He represented his clients so well that he gained a reputation as an able lawyer. But his temper lost yet another opportunity. During an argument with one of his clients, Sanders attacked the man right in the courtroom. The sheriff slapped the handcuffs on Sanders and his career as a lawyer was finished. At age 31, he had to send his wife and children to live with her parents while he went back to the sweaty, back-breaking labor of laying rails and driving spikes for the railroad. The constant turmoil he created with his career changes put a great strain on his marriage that would, many years later, end in divorce.

THE GREAT TALKER

After his short but memorable success as a lawyer, Sanders was confident he could do great things if only he found the right opportunities and kept out of trouble. He found the perfect outlet for his talkative, persistent personality: sales. He racked up impressive sales for an insurance company but once again lasted only 13 months before he lost his temper and was fired.

If Sanders was ever to last long enough in a career to amount to anything, he would have to find work where he could be his own boss so he could not be fired. In the early 1920s, he started a ferry-boat service across the Ohio River between New Albany, Indiana, and Louisville, Kentucky. The business prospered. For the first time in his life, he had money and respect.

But running a ferry-boat company was not enough for him. He was determined to accomplish bigger things. Unfortunately, his stint as executive secretary of the Columbus, Indiana, Chamber of Commerce did not go well. Then he lost a large investment on his plan to manufacture lamps for farms. Short on cash, Sanders had to go back to work for someone else—this time as a salesman for Michelin tires. It was here that Sanders's flair for showmanship emerged. He attracted enormous publicity for his product by staging spectacular contests in which he would pump air into a Michelin tire and a rival tire to see which blew up first. His tires usually won, which greatly helped his sales.

Sanders then branched out into the gasoline business. His relentless promotions and good service— he wiped windshields and checked air in motorists' tires—soon made his brand-new filling station the talk of Nicholasville, Kentucky, a town near the state capitol of Lexington. Everybody in town knew Sanders. According to a neighbor, "Sanders was a great talker. You could always go down there and he would be arguing with somebody about something." Within six months his station was selling more gasoline than any other station in the state.

NOT A DECENT PLACE TO EAT

Sanders' roller coaster life went for another wild ride in the late 1920s when farm prices fell and a severe drought struck the region. Farmers no longer had the money to buy gas, so his station went bankrupt. In 1930, Shell Oil Company offered Sanders a new gas station downstate in Corbin, on the heavily traveled U.S. Highway 25.

While Sanders was ringing up a sale one day, an out-of-town customer complained that there was no decent place to eat in the area. Always alert for a way to increase sales, Sanders cleaned up a storage room at the service station and installed his family's dining table and six chairs. Sanders, who had been improving his cooking by trial and error ever since he was seven, fixed a large dinner at noon. If his gasoline customers happened to be looking for a meal, he served them. If not, his family ate it.

Fast Chicken

The noon dinner grew so popular that Harland Sanders changed the name of his operation to Sanders Cafe and Service Station. Customers soon overflowed his tiny dining room. In 1934, he bought a larger filling station across the street and completely remodeled it to include a six-table dining area. His menu varied from day to day, gradually evolving to feature

Sanders later added motel units to his restaurant and gas station, and changed the name a second time to Sanders Court and Cafe.

SANDERS COURT & CAFE

CORBIN ——— KENTUCKY

Corbin, Ky
Junct. U. S. 25, 25E and 25W
32 Rooms — 32 Baths
At Asheville, N. C.
5 Miles North
At Junct. U. S. 25, 70, 19 and 23

the dishes that customers complimented the most. Among these was his chicken recipe. Many restaurants served chicken without seasoning, assuming patrons would add salt and pepper as they wished. Sanders, however, experimented with adding different spices while he cooked the chicken.

In the late 1930s, a hardware salesman in Corbin invited Sanders into his store one day to show him a new cooking device called a pressure cooker. Vegetables, he pointed out to Sanders, cooked much faster in a pressure cooker than in a pot or pan. Not only would that save time, but the vegetables also tasted better. Sanders bought a pressure cooker. After using it on vegetables with success, he wondered if it would work with chicken. If so, it would solve a major problem with chicken. Because the meat took so long to cook, he had to prepare it well ahead of time. But he had no idea how many of his customers would order chicken. Just to be safe, he prepared more than he needed and that sometimes went to waste. If a pressure cooker could cut the cooking time to a few minutes, he would not have to prepare it so far ahead.

pressure cooker: an airtight metal pot with a locking lid that uses steam under pressure at high temperature to cook food quickly. A gauge that measures the internal pressure fits over a valve on the lid.

Sanders's first tries with pressure-cooked chicken, however, were utter failures. Only after several years of experimentation was he able to work out a method that worked. By cooking in oil at 250 degrees Fahrenheit at 15 pounds of pressure, he could produce tasty chicken—fast.

Although his customers raved about the chicken, Sanders was a perfectionist who kept searching for a way to make it better. It was not until 1952 that he

The Colonel's original recipe of 11 herbs and spices remains a carefully guarded secret, locked in a safe in Louisville, Kentucky. Two different companies each supply half of the ingredients. A computer processing system then blends everything.

finally settled on the mixture of 11 herbs and spices that came to be his trademark.

THE COLONEL

Sanders Cafe was a roaring success throughout the late 1930s and 1940s. So many customers flocked in for one of his home-cooked meals that he eventually expanded his seating to 142.

Sanders thoroughly enjoyed his status as a well-to-do local celebrity. According to one of his friends, John Y. Brown Sr., "Sanders didn't just daydream, like other men. His dreams ate him up." In the mid-1940s, Sanders undertook some ambitious dreams. He founded a special school to train returning World War II veterans to be bricklayers and another one to train airplane pilots. Both projects failed. But for his efforts both as a successful businessman and a community leader, in 1949 Sanders received an honorary colonel's commission from the governor of Kentucky. He had actually been honored earlier with a colonel's commission in 1935, but had never used the title this tradition granted him and had even lost the proclamation paper.

This time, however, Sanders played up his commission to the hilt. From that time on, he referred to himself as Colonel Sanders. His barber suggested that, as long as he was playing the role, he should wear the costume of the old stereotyped Kentucky colonel: a white suit and black string tie. Sanders decided he liked this idea and he began wearing the white suit everywhere. While still hot-tempered and demanding of his employees, he played the role of the charming Southern gentleman in public.

That same year, 1949, Sanders married Claudia Leddington, who had worked for him since 1932. Harland and Josephine had divorced two years earlier, after a long but often unhappy marriage that included the death of their only son, Harland Jr., when he was just 19 years old.

FREEWAY DISASTER

Unlike many owners of popular restaurants at that time, Sanders made no attempt to franchise his Sanders Cafe, although he had tried to establish

Harland Sanders called his second wife "my sweet Claudie." They were still happy together when this picture was taken on Sanders's 89th birthday.

additional restaurants in other cities. But while on a trip to the West Coast in 1952, he stopped in to visit Pete Harman, a friend who lived in Salt Lake City. As owner of the Dew Drop Inn, Harman was always on the lookout for new items to add to his menu. Sanders offered to cook his chicken recipe for the Harman family. After Harman declared it the best he had ever tasted, Sanders showed him how to make it in exchange for a fee. That was the Colonel's first hint that he could make money franchising his recipe, which he had begun to call "Colonel Sanders' Kentucky Fried Chicken."

Sanders tried the same tactic of pressure-cooking chicken and then offering a franchising agreement to restaurant operators back home in the Corbin area. Although he enjoyed only limited success, he was not worried. With his restaurant still going strong in Corbin, he had no financial worries. The restaurant was worth at least the $164,000 that an investor offered him for it in 1953. Anticipating that the new Interstate Highway 75 being constructed near the old Highway 25 route would bring more business than ever to Corbin, Sanders decided to hold off and watch the value of his real estate increase.

Unfortunately, the federal government changed the route of Interstate 75 so that it passed seven miles to the west of Corbin. Instead of bringing more business to Sanders, the new highway drained all the traffic away. When he reached age 65 and was ready to retire, the place was losing money fast. Sanders auctioned all his property, receiving only $75,000.

For Dinner Tonight
CKET O' CHICKEN
TAKE HOME $350 SERVES 5
ARMAN CAFES
Kentucky FRIED CHICKEN

ON THE ROAD AGAIN

The Colonel and his first franchisee, Pete Harman

With less than half the profit that Sanders had anticipated from the sale of his business, he suddenly found himself looking at franchising more seriously. In 1956, after receiving his first Social Security check for $105, the Colonel packed his white Cadillac with a pressure cooker, timers, and his prepackaged herbs and spices, and set out to license his chicken recipe to as many restaurants as he could visit. He scouted out potential franchisees by stopping at restaurants that looked reasonably attractive and ordering their food. Then, dressed in his white suit with string tie and sporting his distinctive white goatee, he dropped in on the manager with his standard offer. He would cook for the help if they would consider adding his Kentucky Fried Chicken to their menu.

In many places, the Colonel had to use all of his sweet-talking charm to get the manager to let him in the door. Many restaurants simply did not believe that enough customers were interested in chicken to justify paying for a recipe. Others were suspicious of this odd character in the white suit. But eventually Sanders won over converts to his recipe. He did business the old fashioned way—sealing a contract with a handshake instead of a long legal document.

For several years, Sanders kept up an exhausting schedule. He spent 90 percent of his time on the road, cooking his chicken and trying to make sales. As customers grew to like this chicken, Sanders's job became easier. Restaurant owners began coming to his makeshift office in Shelbyville, Kentucky, to ask if they could franchise his chicken recipe. By the end of 1960 more than 200 outlets, including some in other countries, were selling his product, each paying him a royalty of five cents for each chicken sold. Sanders was taking in over $100,000 annually in profits. Within a year or so, he decided he had had enough of sleeping in motels. From then on, anyone who wanted to purchase a Kentucky Fried Chicken franchise would have to visit him. Incredibly, even with no sales force he added 100 more outlets by 1963.

A CELEBRITY AT LAST

Managing the handshake deals, food distribution center, and financial records of such a large far-flung enterprise became more than Harland Sanders could manage. Needing a lawyer, he turned to John Y. Brown Jr., the son of his long-time friend. As Brown looked into the operation, he saw possibilities for a huge national franchise system. But he also saw a glaring weakness in Sanders's business. It was entirely a one-man show that depended on the personality and salesmanship of a man in his mid-70s. If something were to happen to Sanders, the business was finished.

Brown offered to buy out Sanders's interest in Kentucky Fried Chicken franchises. Realizing that the Colonel's eccentric personality made him a public relations gold mine, he offered him the opportunity to play the celebrity role he had long sought. Sanders's new position would be to travel around the country and promote his chicken.

Sanders snarled and raged at Brown's plan to take control of the business he had started from scratch. But eventually he came to realize that his business had outgrown him. In February 1964, Sanders sold Kentucky Fried Chicken to Brown and his partner, Jack Massey, for $2 million. Sanders retained the Canadian and British franchises.

After purchasing Kentucky Fried Chicken, John Y. Brown Jr. called Harland Sanders "our ace. He wasn't just somebody that an adman had made up, like Aunt Jemima, or Betty Crocker. He was a real, live human being, and a colorful, attractive, persuasive one. My job was to get him before the American people and let him sell his own product."

A modern KFC restaurant (left) and a typical chicken dinner served there

As Brown had expected, Colonel Sanders soon became a national sales star. He appeared on about 30 national television shows such as "What's My Line?" and "The Tonight Show," charming the host and the audience. He demonstrated a natural gift for acting in television ads promoting his "finger-lickin' good" chicken. With each appearance of the white-suited old Southern gentleman, Kentucky Fried Chicken sales rose.

Brown began franchising carryout stores. All were decked out in red and white colors and featured a portrait of the famous Colonel on their sign. Whereas Kentucky Fried Chicken had previously been just one menu item among many that a restaurant might serve, Brown now insisted that all franchises serve only Kentucky Fried Chicken products. By 1967, 30 percent of all KFC chicken was sold at carryout establishments. At the same time, Brown expanded the menu to include such items as a new extra crispy recipe.

Colonel Sanders fumed at many of these changes. He was peeved with the crispy chicken recipe because it was not his, and he publicly denounced a new gravy that his company introduced. Brown was smart enough not to take offense. If Sanders was outspoken and even ornery, that was all part of the image of this strong-willed old gentleman who was the very symbol of the enterprise.

Brown's clever marketing and Sanders's unique personality made them both rich. Although other chicken-serving competitors cropped up, none of them came close to challenging the identity of the man in the white suit. In 1966, Kentucky Fried Chicken racked up more than $15 million in sales. The company began selling stock to the public in 1966. Three years later, it was listed on the New York Stock Exchange and the Colonel purchased the first 100 shares. In 1970, the company had 3,000 outlets in 48 different countries; by 1997 that figure was up to 10,000 stores in 76 countries.

LEGACY

Harland Sanders continued to serve as a spokesman and good-will ambassador for Kentucky Fried Chicken throughout the 1970s. He also devoted time and money to charities, especially those that helped children, for he had never forgotten his own hard childhood. The March of Dimes was one of his favorites. He stayed active until he died of leukemia in 1980, at the age of 90.

The company Sanders started has changed hands several times. In 1971, John Brown sold out to Heublein, Inc., which was in turn acquired by R. J.

In 1977, Colonel Sanders demonstrated the proper way to fry chicken for Robert Poindexter, a new franchise owner, at KFC's School of Restaurant Management in Louisville.

Reynolds Industries (later RJR Nabisco). In 1986, PepsiCo bought KFC for approximately $840 million. PepsiCo also owned Taco Bell and Pizza Hut and, in 1997, spun off all three fast-food businesses into an independent restaurant company called Tricon Global Restaurants, Inc. Together, the three have nearly 30,000 outlets in about 100 countries.

Despite all these corporate changes, however, Tricon has gone back to using the Colonel in its advertising. Reintroduced in 1998, this cartoon version of Sanders, while youthful, kept his trademark drawl, goatee, white suit, and string tie, reminding people that the company he began still "does chicken right." Sales increased by four percent after the cartoon Colonel debuted.

Sanders almost single-handedly put chicken on the menus of fast-food restaurants. His experiments with the pressure cooker and his use of a premixed batch of seasoning made it possible for something approaching home-cooked chicken to be made quickly enough to meet the demands of the fast-food industry.

With his costume and gentlemanly charm, Harland Sanders also created one of the most memorable images in the history of fast-food marketing. John Brown and Jack Massey had the business sense to turn Kentucky Fried Chicken into a profitable enterprise, and the succeeding owners have successfully continued their work. But KFC could not have dominated fast-food chicken without Sanders to help his company stand out in the public mind above all other competitors.

7

TOM MONAGHAN

DRIVEN TO DELIVER
AT DOMINO'S

In the latter decades of the twentieth century, pizza broke out of the pack of favorite meals to become, far and away, the most popular food of teenagers in the United States. While nearly everyone associates pizza with Italy, the dish that young Americans crave is actually a far cry from the original food that first appeared in Naples, Italy, in the sixteenth century. Pizza developed among the poor, who used bread to pad their meager ingredients into a more substantial meal. The wealthier members of society would not touch it.

Pizza made its first documented appearance in United States restaurants in New York City in 1888. A small store called Little Italy was the first to specialize in pizza. After opening in 1895, it gained

Tom Monaghan (b. 1937) once dreamed of becoming an architect, but instead built a business empire.

popularity among the city's Italian population but attracted little interest beyond that. Ironically, pizza in the form we know it today first won broad acceptance in the Midwest, where relatively few Americans of Italian descent live.

Tom Monaghan was one of the first to recognize the hold that pizza was gaining on young Americans. Not only did he help bring pizza into the mainstream of the fast-food business, but he also found a way to provide a service even more convenient than the McDonald brothers' no-wait service windows.

UNCONTROLLABLE

Thomas S. Monaghan, who was born on March 25, 1937, struggled through a difficult childhood. His father, a truck driver, died when Tom was four. Faced with unexpected financial responsibilities, his mother enrolled in school to become a registered nurse. Trying to care for her two active sons while working and going to school overwhelmed her. Tom spent some time in foster homes and then stayed at St. Joseph's Home For Boys in Jackson, Michigan.

After more than six years under the firm but gentle care of the nuns, he finally rejoined his mother, now employed as a nurse in a hospital in Traverse City, Michigan. But by this time they had grown apart. Fights between the two grew so routine that Tom was soon back in foster homes, usually with farm families. The pace of farm life appealed to him, even the chores such as milking and pitching hay. For the first time, he began to think seriously about his life. As a ninth grader, he made up his mind to become a priest. A few years later he was accepted into a seminary in Grand Rapids.

Unfortunately, Tom did not take seminary rules seriously and he was expelled after less than a year. He returned to live with his mother, his dreams for the future in ashes. His lack of discipline continued to cause problems. Once, when he borrowed the car without telling his mom, she called the police. Tom ended up spending a night in jail over the incident. Continued clashes between mother and son exhausted his mother's patience. She signed an order to place him in a detention home. He spent a miserable six months there, fighting with juvenile delinquents, before his Aunt Peg found out about it and gained custody of him. Tom finished high school living with Peg and Dan Mahler, and their daughter, Maureen, in Ann Arbor.

STUCK WITH A PIZZA PLACE

Despite mediocre grades, Monaghan set his sights on becoming an architect. Before he could begin his studies, however, he needed to earn money to pay his college tuition. A couple of years in the army would provide him the nest egg he needed. Monaghan enlisted with what he mistakenly thought was a U.S. Army recruiter and found himself in the Marines. For a young man who had trouble following the rules, the ultra-disciplined Marine Corps was a miserable experience. But he stuck it out and earned his college money.

While returning to Camp Pendleton, California, after a weekend pass to Las Vegas, he hitched a ride with an oil promoter. The man was such a slick salesman that he talked Monaghan into investing all his college savings in an oil-drilling scheme. Monaghan never saw the man or his money again. When he was discharged from the Marines a few months later, he was right back where he had started—needing to earn money for college.

Tom returned to Ann Arbor and moved in with his brother, Jim. In addition to his job at the post office, Jim worked part-time at DomiNick's, a convenience store owned by Dominick DiVarti that sold pizza and submarine sandwiches. Jim found out that a second DomiNick's store in Ypsilanti, Michigan, was not doing well, and DiVarti was willing to sell it. Jim asked Tom to go in with him to buy the place. The asking price was $500, plus they would have to assume a few thousand dollars of debt that the store had accumulated.

Tom, who had been running a newsstand since his return to Ann Arbor in the summer of 1959, agreed to the plan. On December 9, 1960, the brothers took over the little shop on the edge of the Eastern Michigan University campus. At the time, Tom knew next to nothing about pizza. He had not even liked the few tastes of pizza he had had as a teenager. But now that he owned DomiNick's, he set out to learn how to make the best pizza he could. DiVarti showed him how to mix the dough and toss the pizza crust. He also informed him that "the secret of good pizza is in the sauce." Taking his advice seriously, Monaghan set out looking for a sauce recipe even better than DiVarti's.

Over 20 years after he opened his first restaurant, Tom Monaghan could still bake a tempting pizza.

At first, it appeared that this business venture would be as futile as the money he had thrown away on the oil con man. The Monaghan brothers had room for only two tables, which meant they had to count on carryout and delivery for much of their sales. They did not even have a telephone to take orders for the first month. The brothers sold $99 worth of pizza their first week. Business picked up slowly after that, but Tom and Jim often argued about how to run the store. Only eight months after they opened, Jim decided to pull out. He did not have the time both to run the store and keep his post office job.

Suddenly Tom faced a difficult choice: Sell the store and continue his quest to become an architect, or run the business himself and forgo college. He chose to move into an apartment across the street from the store and stay in business.

FOCUS ON DELIVERY

After the rocky start, sales began to pick up in the spring. But just when Monaghan began to have hope for the shop, classes ended at the university and business plummeted again. Monaghan knew he had to make some drastic changes to turn a profit. He eliminated the sub sandwiches to concentrate only on pizza. Then he axed DomiNick's featured item: the 6-inch individual pizzas. Monaghan realized that he could make and deliver a 12-inch pizza in the same amount of time as a 6-inch. Selling only 12-inch pizzas would greatly increase the total amount of pizza he could make in an evening. He also found the special sauce he was seeking in an old Italian restaurant in Lansing.

While building up business at DomiNick's, Monaghan learned that a pizza parlor in Mount Pleasant, Michigan, was failing. Upon investigation, he discovered two useful bits of information.

First, the store was located near Central Michigan University. Monaghan knew from experience that college students ordered more pizza than anyone. And second, the store did not offer free delivery. Monaghan believed that he could make the place successful simply by offering that service. He bought the store and renamed it Pizza King. While making his first personal delivery of a pizza to a Central

Hungry college students contributed to the success of Domino's.

Michigan dormitory, he met his future wife, Marjorie Zybach, who had by chance filled in for a friend at the reception desk that evening.

Continuing to focus on college students, Tom Monaghan, with help from a partner, opened a Pizza King in Ann Arbor, home of the University of Michigan, in May 1962. Once again, he emphasized reliable delivery service. Meanwhile, back in Ypsilanti, he moved the original DomiNick's to a better location and opened a new store on the other side of town. He could cover the delivery area much more easily with two pizza places.

But the new store was too small to house a full kitchen, so Monaghan prepared pizza dough and toppings for both places in the larger store. He soon saw that this system of making pizzas in a central location had many advantages. This was the beginning of the commissary system that would later supply all Monaghan's outlets. He also decided to eliminate sit-down service completely and make free delivery his trademark.

At about that time, Dominick DiVarti asked Monaghan to stop using the name DomiNick's. Monaghan, who was already bothered by having some stores named DomiNick's and others Pizza King, had to come up with something new. He considered hundreds of new names and was leaning toward Pinocchio's when a delivery boy suggested he alter the old name just slightly to Domino's.

Monaghan had to scrimp to keep his struggling group of pizza stores in business. He and Margie were married in August 1962, and they set up their

home in a house trailer. After their first two daugh-
ters were born, Margie Monaghan helped with the
bookkeeping. The little girls sometimes slept in
cardboard boxes in a corner of a room at the
Ypsilanti store while Margie worked. Tom worked
long hours, often staying on the job until 4 A.M. and
then starting again at 10 the next morning, seven
days a week.

*Domino's was the first pizza
company to use car signs
and hot bags, and to promise fast delivery.*

BUILDING SALES

Tom Monaghan was not a trained businessman and he ran a loose ship. He had no manual or operating procedures. He had only three basic rules: all employees had to be on time, work one weekend night, and never just sit around. Monaghan's tough childhood had taught him to take care of his own problems. When customers refused to pay or mistreated his delivery people, he showed up himself to settle the problem, occasionally with his fists.

Constantly on the lookout for ways to improve his business, he traveled to the most famous pizzerias in the country. He was surprised by the poor service and inconsistent quality of even the best places. For the first time, he realized that the door was wide open for a well-run, quality pizza chain to take the country by storm. Domino's, he decided, would be that chain.

Monaghan spent a great deal of money working on improving his business. "Any idiot can cut costs," he declared. "But you can't always build sales and that's what I'm doing." He invested in better pizza-making equipment and the world's largest pizza oven, capable of baking 90 twelve-inch pizzas at a time. He spent much time and research on boxes that could hold their shape so the pizzas would not be crushed when stacked. He started conducting independent taste tests to measure the quality of his product.

Monaghan's aggressive policy ran aground, however, when a partner whom he had teamed up with when he expanded into Ann Arbor declared bank-ruptcy in 1966. Monaghan had to assume $75,000 of the partner's debt, and the extra load nearly ruined him. But a franchising program helped him claw his way back to financial soundness. Investors could purchase 50 percent of a franchise, with the owner-manager purchasing 25 percent, and Domino's owning the remaining 25 percent. In addition, Domino's charged franchises a percentage of sales in exchange for providing pizza ingredients and other supplies.

Business was so good in 1967 that the Monaghans were able to buy their first house. After signing up five new franchises in early 1968, Monaghan thought he was finally on his way to success. But then on February 8, 1968, fire destroyed the Domino's office and commissary—the main kitchen that supplied all the other stores. Suddenly all his stores, including the new franchises, had to scramble for materials and pizza ingredients. Worse yet, his insurance paid only $13,000 of the $150,000 worth of damage.

MORE DISASTER

After recovering from this loss, Monaghan made a nearly disastrous business move. In its early days, Domino's catered almost exclusively to college campuses. Monaghan was so focused on the college market that he knew within 10 percent how many students lived in dorms in every college in the country. In 1969, however, he decided to expand into residential neighborhoods. Typically, he went all-out before testing the waters. In the first 10 months of 1969, he opened 32 new stores. The strategy backfired. Domino's guarantee of 30-minute service was not enough to help his stores compete with established pizzerias that offered a wider variety of menu items. During the first year, most of the new stores did only one-tenth the amount of business Monaghan had expected. At the same time, he lost all of his records when switching over to a new computer accounting system.

Checks began bouncing, bills went unpaid. Domino's fell behind in paying sales taxes and withholding taxes, and the taxes then multiplied because of penalties and interest. Monaghan found himself over $1 million in debt. He had to sell company stock, even his own furniture, and he slept in his car when on the road to save motel expenses. Some Domino's stores were closed and employees laid off. Monaghan pleaded with franchise owners not to sue Domino's for breach of contract.

Again, Monaghan worked tirelessly to climb out of debt and win back the confidence of investors and franchise owners. Learning from his mistakes, he began to take a more active role in managing the franchise system. He placed a greater emphasis on recruiting and training talented managers and on visiting the stores in person to check on progress.

Tom Monaghan weathered the storm that saw his franchise chain drop from 115 stores to 69. By September 1977, he was able to pay off the last dollar of debt. Domino's began expanding again, reaching 200 stores by the end of 1978 and 440 in 1980. Domino's opened store number 1,000 in 1983.

A MODERN DAY BARNUM

One of Monaghan's heroes was the legendary circus showman P. T. Barnum. Monaghan's own flair for showmanship helped him establish an identity for his often floundering business. For example, following the Detroit Tigers' victory in the 1968 World Series, a huge crowd of fans gathered at the airport to welcome the heroes home from St. Louis. "When the Tigers won it, I was struck by the idea that we had to give the players some hot Domino's pizzas in celebration," said Monaghan. He had 100 pizzas baked and put in portable sterno heaters, and he and a colleague rushed toward the airport 20 minutes away. When a massive traffic jam of Tigers fans prevented them from reaching the airport, Tom Monaghan shifted gears and sold all 100 pizzas to the people stuck on the freeway. "And we had so much fun doing it that we didn't regret missing the players," he recalled.

Then one of his franchise owners scheduled a special promotion for the last Sunday in January without realizing it was Super Bowl Sunday. The store was buried under an avalanche of orders they could not possibly fill. Monaghan learned from the experience and scheduled a Super Sunday for the following year. This time the store was prepared, and it delivered 1,000 pizzas an hour for five hours straight. The gimmick caught the interest of the news media, providing Domino's with national publicity.

In the mid-1970s, Monaghan came up with his Mystery Customer Program. Instead of sending managers around to check on the stores, he recruited customers to evaluate the company's products and services in exchange for discounted prices on pizza.

REACHING THE TOP

Monaghan had to survive yet another scare in the 1970s when Amstar Corporation challenged his company name in a lawsuit. Amstar had been using the brand name Domino for its sugar long before Domino's pizza came along. Monaghan thought about changing the name, but in the end he just could not walk away from a fight. The court battle dragged on for five years. In 1979, a judge gave Monaghan three months to change the name of his franchises. But in 1980 he won an appeal of the verdict. Upon hearing the decision he was so relieved he broke down and sobbed.

Domino's made so much money for Monaghan that he was able to fulfill a boyhood dream by purchasing the Detroit Tigers baseball team in 1983. But one last challenge remained. In 1985, Domino's had grown large enough to attract the notice of the giant pizza restaurant chain, Pizza Hut. Officials at Pizza Hut decided to challenge Domino's for dominance in the delivery market, which had previously been only a small part of its business. It announced plans to open 1,000 new pizza delivery stores. Although Pizza Hut does enjoy a larger slice of the total pizza market, its aggressive drive failed to dislodge Domino's from its delivery dominance.

Monaghan loved meeting the players and spending time at the Tigers' spring training headquarters in Florida. He's pictured here on one such visit in 1984 with club president James Campbell (left) and Tigers manager Sparky Anderson (center).

New Pizza on the Block: Papa John's

John Schnatter, founder of Papa John's chain of pizzerias, began making pizzas while still in high school in Jeffersonville, Indiana. After he graduated from college in 1983, he cleaned out a broom closet in his father's tavern, sold his beloved 1972 Camaro to purchase used restaurant equipment, and began making pizza. The customers loved it! Two years later, he opened the first Papa John's restaurant.

Schnatter's goal was to fill a void he thought existed in the national pizza chains: superior-quality traditional pizza that could be delivered. During the mid-1990s, he challenged the established pizza chains with his "better ingredients, better pizza." Ranked third in sales among pizza franchises in 2000, Papa John's has grown at double-digit rates, making it the fastest-growing pizza company in America.

Although still number one in sales, during the 1990s Pizza Hut closed hundreds of marginal stores. Little Caesar's market share declined, putting it in fourth place. Domino's retained a steady second place. By 2000, Papa John's had more than 2,200 restaurants in the United States and five international markets. The company's corporate offices are in Louisville, Kentucky.

John Schnatter successfully challenged the established pizza chains.

LEGACY

Tom Monaghan provided the ultimate in fast-food service by focusing his energy on delivery. Early in his career, he set a goal of handing a hot pizza to customers within 30 minutes of their order. By 1967, he officially announced that goal as a company policy. Then he set about making sure that Domino's could back up their promise. Because of his speedy service priority, customers could get a tasty, inexpensive meal in a hurry without ever having to leave the comfort of their homes.

The 30-minute delivery promise and a flair for promotion helped Monaghan build and rebuild his business time and time again. So did innovations like the sturdy, corrugated pizza box, the commissary supply system, and the electric heated hot bags the company introduced in 1998. Starting from a single store in Ypsilanti, Michigan, Domino's has grown to an enterprise that in 2000 included over 6,000 stores that deliver more than 6 million pizzas a week.

In September 1998, Tom Monaghan retired to devote himself to the many Catholic charities he supported. Bain Capital, Inc., acquired a 93 percent stake in Domino's from Monaghan and his family. The company, headed in 2000 by Chief Executive Officer David Brandon at corporate headquarters in Ann Arbor, Michigan, remains a profitable contender among the several national pizza franchises.

"McDonald's is my model, and Mr. Kroc is my hero," Monaghan declared. After 12 years of phone calls, he finally wangled an appointment to meet the king of franchising. Their meeting, scheduled for 15 minutes, lasted over two hours, Monaghan said, because Kroc kept asking "such great questions" about Domino's operations. That evening, an excited Domino's store owner in San Diego called Monaghan to report that Ray Kroc had just come in and ordered a pizza.

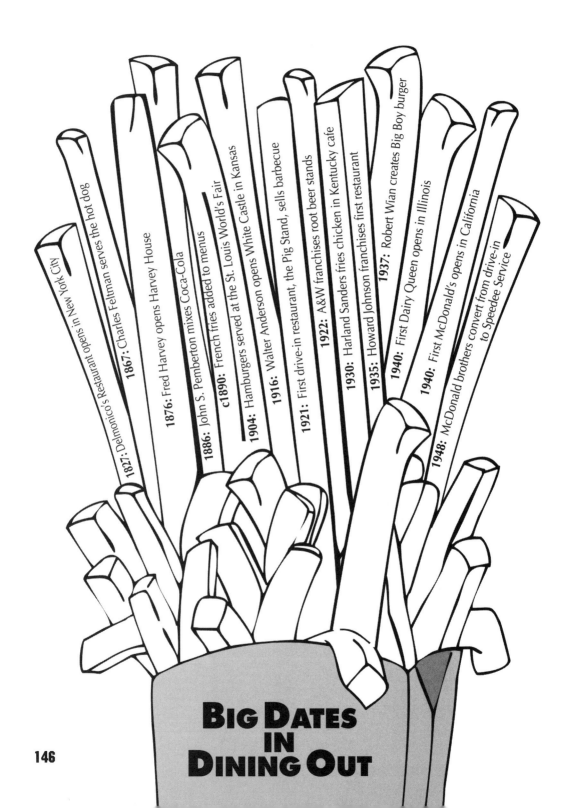

1827: Delmonico's Restaurant opens in New York City

1867: Charles Feltman serves the hot dog

1876: Fred Harvey opens Harvey House

1886: John S. Pemberton mixes Coca-Cola

c1890: French fries added to menus

1904: Hamburgers served at the St. Louis World's Fair

1916: Walter Anderson opens White Castle in Kansas

1921: First drive-in restaurant, the Pig Stand, sells barbecue

1922: A&W franchises root beer stands

1930: Harland Sanders fries chicken in Kentucky cafe

1935: Howard Johnson franchises first restaurant

1937: Robert Wian creates Big Boy burger

1940: First Dairy Queen opens in Illinois

1940: First McDonald's opens in California

1948: McDonald brothers convert from drive-in to Speedee Service

BIG DATES IN DINING OUT

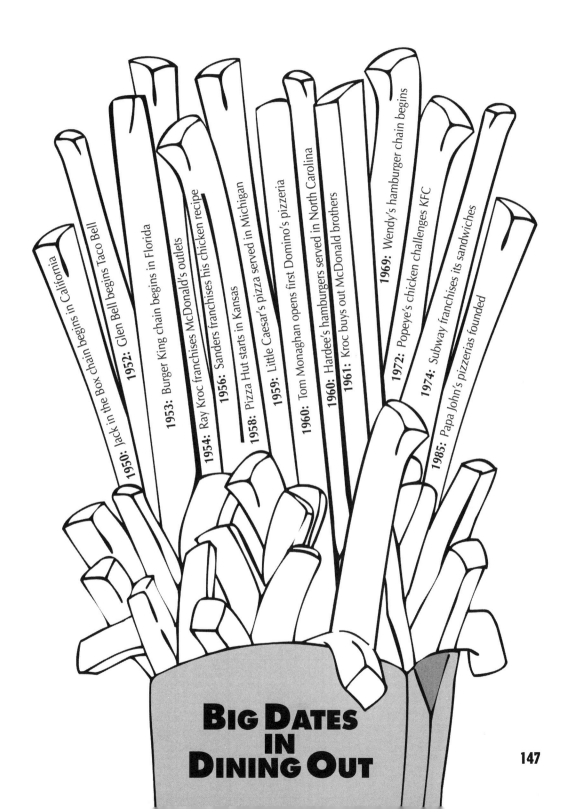

1950: Jack in the Box chain begins in California

1952: Glen Bell begins Taco Bell

1953: Burger King chain begins in Florida

1954: Ray Kroc franchises McDonald's outlets

1956: Sanders franchises his chicken recipe

1958: Pizza Hut starts in Kansas

1959: Little Caesar's pizza served in Michigan

1960: Tom Monaghan opens first Domino's pizzeria

1960: Hardee's hamburgers served in North Carolina

1961: Kroc buys out McDonald brothers

1969: Wendy's hamburger chain begins

1972: Popeye's chicken challenges KFC

1974: Subway franchises its sandwiches

1985: Papa John's pizzerias founded

BIG DATES IN DINING OUT

GLOSSARY

boarding house: a house where paying guests receive meals and a room

carhop: a waitress or waiter who serves customers parked in their cars outside of a restaurant

chain restaurant or **store:** an individual outlet that is a part of a group of similar stores or restaurants with the same management and ownership

corporation: a business that is a legal entity, chartered by a state or the federal government, and separate and distinct from the persons who own it. Considered an artificial person by the court, a corporation may own property, incur debts, sue, or be sued. Its chief features are limited liability (owners can lose only what they invest), transfer of ownership through the sales of shares of stock, and centralized management.

diner: a term coined by Patrick Tierney of New Rochelle, New York, who wanted to upgrade the lunch wagon into something that more resembled a railroad dining car. Although the word is often applied to small restaurants or main street cafes, a true diner is a long, modular building that can be towed from place to place.

Dow Jones Industrials: a group of large companies whose daily stock prices are averaged to measure the movement of the stock market. The companies are chosen by Dow Jones, a respected financial information services firm that publishes *The Wall Street Journal* and *Barron's,* to be representative of American business.

drive-in restaurant: a restaurant at which motorists park in a parking lot and are served in their cars. A **drive-up** customer parks and walks up to a service window inside or outside of the restaurant to order. Restaurants with **drive-through** service feature outdoor menus and microphones so customers can order their meals, then drive past a window where they pay and pick up their food without ever having left their vehicles.

eating houses: businesses serving food. This name was used before the term "restaurant" became popular in the 1800s.

franchise: a licensing arrangement in which an investor pays money to the owner of a particular brand-name product or business for permission to sell that product or operate that business in a certain territory. The person offering the permission is called the **franchiser**. The person buying the rights is the **franchisee**.

going public: offering shares of stock of a privately owned company to the public for the first time

industrial revolution: the term applied to the social and economic change from an agricultural society to a modern industrial one made possible by machine production of goods and other technological advances. In the United States, this rapid transition from farm to factory occurred largely after the Civil War ended in 1865.

inn: *see* **tavern**

lunch wagon: a wagon that a proprietor would take from place to place to serve food, usually to factory workers. Early wagons used a service window; later models offered a counter inside the wagon so customers were sheltered from bad weather. Lunch wagons were manufactured by several different companies during the late 1800s.

menu: a list of dishes served or available for a meal in a restaurant, either printed for individual use or written on a large display

New York Stock Exchange: the oldest and largest stock exchange in the U.S., established in 1792. Located on Wall Street in New York City, the NYSE trades more than 2,600 stocks, and each company must meet the exchange's strict listing requirements.

oyster houses: eating houses that specialized in serving oysters preserved and shipped in salt brine. Oyster houses were a craze of the 1800s. Inexpensive and plentiful, oysters offered an exotic addition to the bland diet most people ate. Pollutants have since destroyed the oyster beds of New England and reduced those of Chesapeake Bay, making oysters a more expensive delicacy today.

pressure cooker: an airtight metal pot with a locking lid that uses steam under pressure at high temperature to cook food quickly. A gauge that measures the internal pressure fits over a valve on the lid.

public offering: soliciting the general public for the sale of investment units. It generally requires approval by the Securities and Exchange Commission and/or state securities agencies.

restaurant: a place where meals are served to the public, from the French word *restaurer*, to restore

stock market: an organized market where stocks and bonds are actively traded

tavern or **inn:** an establishment licensed to sell alcoholic beverages to customers on the premises. During the eighteenth and nineteenth centuries in America, taverns also often offered meals and lodging to travelers.

BIBLIOGRAPHY

"About KFC." http://www.kfc.com/AboutKFC/about_main.htm, cited November 23, 1999.

Alexander, Jack. "Howard Johnson: Host of the Highways." *Saturday Evening Post*, July 19, 1958.

"Company Profile." http://www.dominos.com/Press/CompanyProfile.cfm, cited November 26, 1999.

Cox, James A. "How Good Food and Harvey Skirts Won the West." *Smithsonian*, September 1987.

"Domino's Pizza Announces Industry First—Heated Hot Bags." http://www.dominos.com/Press/ViewRelease.cfm?Articleid=55, cited November 26, 1999.

Gellene, Denise. "Advertisers Bring Company Icons Out of Mothballs." Minneapolis *Star Tribune*, August 16, 1999.

Gilpin, Kenneth N. "Richard McDonald, 89, Fast Food Revolutionary." *The New York Times Biographical Service*, July 16, 1998.

Greenwald, John. "Slice, Dice and Devour." *Time*, October 26, 1998.

"History." http://www.papajohns.com/history, cited April 18, 2000.

Hogan, David Gerard. *Selling 'Em By the Sack: White Castle and the Creation of American Food*. New York: New York University Press, 1997.

"Introducing America to Americans: The Fred Harvey Company and Native American Art." http://www.heard.org/exhibits/inventingsw/sft/sft6.html, cited November 30, 1999.

Jakle, John A. and Keith A. Sculle. *Fast Food: Roadside Restaurants in the Automobile Age*. Baltimore: Johns Hopkins University Press, 1999.

Kroc, Ray with Robert Anderson. *Grinding It Out: The Making of McDonald's*. New York: St. Martin's Press, 1987.

Love, John F. *McDonald's: Behind the Arches*. New York: Bantam, 1986.

"The McDonald's Story." http://www.mcdonalds.com/corporate/info/history/history.html, cited November 23, 1999.

Monaghan, Tom with Robert Anderson. *Pizza Tiger*. New York: Random, 1986.

Monninger, Joseph. "Fast Food." *American Heritage*, April 1988.

Otis, Caroline Hall. *The Cone with the Curl on Top*. Minneapolis: International Dairy Queen, 1990.

Pearce, John Edward. *The Colonel*. Garden City, N.Y.: Doubleday, 1982.

Pillsbury, Richard. *From Boarding House to Bistro: The American Restaurant Then and Now*. Cambridge, Mass.: Unwin Hyman, 1990.

Poling-Kempes, Lesley. *The Harvey Girls: Women Who Opened the West*. New York: Paragon House, 1989.

Richman, Alan. "The Real Burger King." *Gentleman's Quarterly*, October 1996.

Stodghill II, Ron. "A Tale of Pizza, Pride and Piety." *Time*, October 26, 1998.

"The Story of Colonel Sanders." http://www.kfc.com/COLONEL/colhistory1.htm, cited November 23, 1999.

SOURCE NOTES

Introduction

p. 16: Joseph Monninger, "Fast Food," *American Heritage* (April 1988), 69.

p. 19: James A. Cox, "How Good Food and Harvey Skirts Won the West," *Smithsonian* (September 1987), 130.

Chapter One

p. 30 (margin): Cox, "How Good Food and Harvey Skirts Won the West," 136.

pp. 30-31: Cox, "How Good Food and Harvey Skirts Won the West," 138.

Chapter Two

p. 41: David Gerard Hogan, *Selling 'Em By the Sack: White Castle and the Creation of American Food* (New York: New York University Press, 1997), 27.

p. 43: Hogan, *Selling 'Em By the Sack*, 32.

p. 45 (margin): Hogan, *Selling 'Em By the Sack*, 31.

p. 47: Hogan, *Selling 'Em By the Sack*, 31.

p. 48 (margin): Hogan, *Selling 'Em by the Sack*, 24.

Chapter Three

p. 59 (first): Caroline Hall Otis, *The Cone with the Curl on Top* (Minneapolis: International Dairy Queen, 1990), 12.

p. 59 (second): Otis, *The Cone with the Curl on Top* ,13.

p. 60 (caption): Otis, *The Cone with the Curl on Top* , 11.

p. 62: Otis, *The Cone with the Curl on Top* , 24.

p. 67: Otis, *The Cone with the Curl on Top* , 34.

p. 73: John A. Jakle and Keith A. Sculle, *Fast Food: Roadside Restaurants in the Automobile Age* (Baltimore: Johns Hopkins University Press, 1999), 196.

Chapter Four

p. 76 (margin): Monninger, "Fast Food," 70.

p. 80: John F. Love, *McDonald's: Behind the Arches* (Toronto: Bantam, 1986), 13.

p. 81: Love, *McDonald's: Behind the Arches*, 14.

p. 88: Love, *McDonald's: Behind the Arches*, 23.

p. 89 (margin): Kenneth N. Gilpin, "Richard McDonald, 89, Fast-Food Revolutionary," *The New York Times Biographical Service* (July 16, 1998), 1090.

Chapter Five

p. 93: Ray Kroc with Robert Anderson, *Grinding It Out* (New York: St. Martin's Press, 1987), 15.

p. 95: Kroc, *Grinding It Out*, 56.

p. 101: Kroc, *Grinding It Out*, 77.

p. 103: Kroc, *Grinding It Out*, 78.

p. 108 (first): Kroc, *Grinding It Out*, photo insert, 13.

p. 108 (second): Love, *McDonald's: Behind the Arches*, 43.

Chapter Six

p. 111: John Edward Pearce, *The Colonel* (Garden City, New York: Doubleday, 1982), 7.

p. 112 (margin): Pearce, *The Colonel*, 4.

p. 115: Pearce, *The Colonel*, 43.

p. 118: Pearce, *The Colonel*, 79.

p. 122 (margin): Pearce, *The Colonel*, 88.

p. 123 (caption): Pearce, *The Colonel*, 137.

Chapter Seven

p. 132: Tom Monaghan with Robert Anderson, *Pizza Tiger* (New York: Random, 1986), 110.

p. 138: Monaghan, *Pizza Tiger*, 50.

p. 141 (first): Monaghan, *Pizza Tiger*, 135.

p. 141 (second): Monaghan, *Pizza Tiger*, 136.

p. 142 (margin): Monaghan, *Pizza Tiger*, 232-233.

p. 145 (margin): Monaghan, *Pizza Tiger*, 247-248.

INDEX

ABOUT THE AUTHOR

Nathan Aaseng is an award-winning author of over 100 fiction and nonfiction books for young readers. He writes on subjects ranging from science and technology to business, government, politics, and law. Nathan Aaseng's books for The Oliver Press include the **Business Builders** series and nine titles in the **Great Decisions** series. He lives with his wife, Linda, and their four children in Eau Claire, Wisconsin.

PHOTO CREDITS